DISCARD

# SAKHAROV SPEAKS

# SAKHAROV

# SPEAKS

ANDREI D. SAKHAROV

Edited and with a Foreword
by HARRISON E. SALISBURY

VINTAGE BOOKS

A Division of Random House
NEW YORK

VINTAGE BOOKS EDITION MAY 1974
*First Edition*

*Library of Congress Catalog Card Number: 73-20729*
*ISBN: 0-394-71302-8*

*Manufactured in the United States of America*

# CONTENTS

# SAKHAROV SPEAKS

# FOREWORD

On June 22, 1941, a thin, tall, blond, shy young student named Andrei Dmitrivich Sakharov had just completed his third year in the physics faculty of Moscow University. At noon on that warm sunshiny day he—like all Russians—was stunned to hear on the radio the voice of Foreign Minister Molotov announcing that Russia was at war, that Germany had attacked before dawn that morning. The immediate impulse of the twenty-year-old Sakharov was to join his classmates in a rush to the colors, to sign up for service in the Soviet armed forces. But this was not to be. Sakharov was regarded as possibly the most brilliant physics student in the memory of the Moscow faculty. He was, in effect, declared a national asset, reserved from military duty. Graduating in 1942, he spent the rest of the war years as an engineer in a military factory. In 1947, at the age of twenty-six, he received a degree of Candidate of Doctor of Science. There is no precise American equivalent of this degree, but it is an academic achievement somewhat comparable to an American Ph.D.

Sakharov's degree was awarded for work in cosmic-ray theory at the famous Lebedev Institute of Physics of the Soviet Academy of Science, where he had joined the "Tamm group," an extraordinary constellation of young physicists who had gathered around the future Nobel laureate Dr. Igor E. Tamm.

The brilliance of young physicists is, of course, axiomatic. Not a few look back from the sturdy age of twenty-six or twenty-seven to say, "My best work was done at twenty-two." Sakharov's genius by no means peaked at twenty-two, but the vigor and creativity of his youthful mind were consistent with the tradition of physics scholarship.

Before he was twenty-seven Sakharov had appeared in the Soviet *Journal of Experimental and Theoretical Physics* with two papers, one on the generation of a hard component of cosmic rays (probably drawn from his doctoral thesis) and another, foreshadowing his new era of concentration, concerning the interaction of electrons and positrons. One more scientific paper under Sakharov's signature was published in 1948. It dealt with the "temperature of excitation in plasma of a gaseous discharge." From then on, silence. For nearly a decade the name of Sakharov vanished. No published research, no papers, no citations. Nothing. It was as though Russia's most promising young scientist had disappeared without a trace.

As we now know, Sakharov did not vanish. He, together with Tamm and others, had been put to work in deepest secrecy developing the principles of the H-bomb, and, indeed, by 1950 Sakharov and Tamm had perfected the method of an electrical discharge in a plasma, placed in a magnetic field, which produces a thermonuclear reaction, i.e., the H-bomb.

For these achievements and others connected with the theory and production of the hydrogen weapon Sakharov was to receive—in secret—the Stalin Prize, three Orders of Socialist Labor (the highest civilian honor in the Soviet Union), and an extraordinary salary fixed by the Kremlin of two thousand rubles a month, about twenty-seven thousand dollars a year at current exchange rates; every possible privilege in living comforts, special housing, chauffeurs, access to restricted consumer goods; and a twenty-four-hour-a-day bodyguard who accompanied him everywhere—even when he went swimming and skiing.

But no one outside a few scientists holding the highest security clearances, the principal officers of the Soviet government, and, of course, of the Ministry of Medium Machine Construction (as the Soviet Union called and still calls its atomic energy agency) knew of the existence of this still thin, still blond, still shy, still incredibly brilliant young man who would at the age of thirty-two be elected in 1953 a full member of the Soviet Academy of Sciences and named a Doctor of Science. He was the youngest man ever so honored, an honor underlined by the fact that in the same year in which he catapulted to full membership his remarkable colleague, Dr. Tamm, after *twenty years* as a corresponding member of the Academy, also was named a full member.

It is obvious that in speaking of Sakharov we are

speaking of one of the great intellects of our age—a man whose name flows easily and naturally into the rhythm of the list of those like Rutherford, Einstein, Bohr, Heisenberg, Kapitsa, and Oppenheimer, whose minds have changed the world.

There is clearly something about the discipline of physics that causes a great physicist to look beyond the formulas, the theorems, the infinitely intricate hypotheses by which he tests and determines the natural laws of the universe and into the seemingly simpler but actually much more complex phenomena of man's society. Or, perhaps, this is an illusion. Perhaps it is simply that with their finely tuned minds the physicists are able to penetrate more swiftly and more deeply the murk and bias with which human beings normally shroud their affairs.

Whatever the cause, it is a fact that after Einstein elaborated his great Theory of Relativity his mind began to struggle with questions of war and peace. Oppenheimer turned from the A-bomb to the deep humanistic implications of the role of a scientist in society. So have many others.

Thus it is not surprising that at the advanced age of thirty-seven Andrei Sakharov, still cloaked by the deepest of security classifications (although he had managed to publish an article on U-meson reaction in hydrogen in the *Journal of Experimental and Theoretical Physics* with his close collaborator Yakov Zeldovich in 1957), began to thrust his thoughts outward—from the intense, narrow world of applied physics and nuclear weapons production and away from the remote center where he and his colleagues conducted their research in monastic seclusion—to the more earthly problems of the society in which he lived.

That process, slowly gathering momentum and steadily broadening in scope, is still going on and, much more than his fathership of the Soviet H-bomb, is why the name Sakharov is today known throughout the world as the symbol of global humanitarianism.

The Russian society that formed and shaped Sakharov had undergone enormous changes even in the brief period of his life. Born in Moscow in 1921, when the flames of civil war and revolution were just flickering out, Sakharov was the son of a physicist, Dmitri Sakharov, well-known, respected, author of a familiar classroom physics text, and a professor at the Lenin Pedagogical Institute. Thus Sakharov was born into a well-known stratum of Russian society, the scientific intelligentsia, and it is this circumstance that has given to his life its characteristic content and luminosity. The Russian *intelligent* has no precise counterpart in other societies. He is not simply a university graduate or an individual given over to intellectual pursuits. He is not, for example, a white-collar man as opposed to a blue-collar man. In fact, it is not his academic or economic status that distinguishes the Russian *intelligent* but, rather, his moral and social outlook, his sense of dedication to principle, to the improvement of the lot of his fellow man, to the elimination of social evils, to selflessness, to the moral imperative of speaking the truth as he believes it, regardless of physical and material consequences. He is imbued, to some extent, by the traditional spirit of Russian universalism. He believes in the perfectability of man and in his own duty to put sacrifice above self. The ideals of the Russian *intelligent* were nourished during the long and bloody years of struggle against the backwardness and tyranny of the Czarist regime. They gave the revolutionary movement moral fervor and philosophical justification. And, as difficult as the Soviet period proved to be, with its police, its repressions, its purges, its propaganda, and its thought control, the unique spirit of the Russian *intelligent,* like a phoenix, has survived.

It was in this milieu of earnest, dedicated, passionately honest, fiercely principled scientists and thinkers, writers and philosophers, that Sakharov's early years were spent and in which, to be certain, he has continued to live during his adult life, even though the strict regulations of Soviet security (not to mention his own fierce concentration on nuclear and cosmic studies) tended to limit the range of his social and personal contacts.

It was probably inevitable that at a certain point a man of Sakharov's upbringing would begin to turn his attention to subjects outside the world of physics. He had been able to morally sustain his intense preoccupation with weapons research and theory in the belief, as he expressed it, that "I was working for peace." At the time he and Tamm began their research on the problem of the H-bomb the Soviet Union had just conducted her first successful A-bomb test (in October 1949). The crash program initiated by Stalin to match the American nuclear breakthrough of 1945 had paid off with startling swiftness under the forced draft of a research and production effort headed by Lavrenti P. Beria, Stalin's notorious chief of secret police. Production of the 1949 A-bomb left Russia far from parity with the huge American nuclear inventory steadily piled up in the years after the war, yet the Soviet A-bomb was a critically important achievement, which gave Russia at least the possibility of nuclear response to an American strike. But much more

was needed if parity in deterrence was to be achieved—
a long-range missile and rocket program (which ultimately gave the Soviets the ICBM and Sputnik) and a
new generation of nuclear weapons, which physicists
knew had to be the H-bomb. It was this achievement
that was attained by Sakharov and Tamm. They had
nothing to do with the A-bomb program or the rocket
program, but in a breakneck race with American scientists the Russian team won. They produced an H-bomb
before the Americans and for the first time gave the Kremlin a guarantee that Russia was now qualitatively ahead
of the United States, even if still far behind quantitatively.

To Sakharov this undertaking was clearly in the
cause of humanity. If, he reasoned, both the United States
and the Soviet Union possessed this terrible nuclear capa-
bility, they would be compelled to draw the logical conclusions—to negotiate their differences rather than destroy
each other and the world. Nourished by this conviction
(which hardly differs from the convictions of many of the
physicists who worked on the American A-bomb, such
as Oppenheimer, Bethe, Szilard, and others), Sakharov
seems to have had no moral problems with his H-bomb
weapons work. In this it should be noted that he differed,
as did Tamm, from the most famous of Russian physicists, Peter Kapitsa, who refused Stalin's request to
work on the A-bomb and, in consequence, was held under
house arrest for a number of years.

The watershed in Sakharov's evolution from brilliant
weapons physicist to concerned Soviet and world citizen
came in 1957–8. By this time Soviet security vis-à-vis the
United States had been assured with the H-bomb and the
ICBM. Soviet international prestige had been raised high

by Sputnik and the Soviet space program, which the United States was now frantically attempting to match. The Chinese even felt that the balance of power had moved to the Communist side and Chairman Mao was confidently proclaiming that "the East Wind prevails over the West Wind." Khrushchev, not so sanguine, was actively preparing for the move toward détente, which was to flower in 1959 with his visit to the United States and the famous "spirit of Camp David."

It was an appropriate moment for thought-taking. In 1958, though still distant from Moscow in the secret Soviet nuclear weapons research center, Sakharov moved out of theory and theorems into the field of politics and policy. He did two things—one private and one public. Privately, for the first time in his career, he sought to influence a major Soviet policy decision. There had been a six-month interval in Soviet atmospheric tests and Sakharov, convinced that further testing in the air was not needed for scientific purposes and would only tend to aggravate the arms race and increase the dangers from fallout, sought to halt a scheduled series of Soviet weapons tests. He managed to convince Igor Kurchatov, then in charge of the program. Kurchatov sought permission from Khrushchev to cancel the sequence. But Khrushchev refused and the tests went on.

In this same year, 1958, Sakharov for the first time took a public stand on a major question of public policy. He and his associate, Zeldovich, wrote a letter raising basic questions about the Soviet educational system and setting forth the principles of a new program for especially gifted children.

It was a moment when the question of educational

reform was in the forefront of discussion. Khrushchev had launched a major drive to subject Soviet education to a strong infusion of what he called "practical" work, reducing the time spent on formal studies and sending youngsters into factories and out into the fields. The educational process would be interrupted at the age of fifteen or sixteen for two or three years of practical work. Khrushchev proposed to make this a mandatory across-the-board regulation except for a few artistic students, such as those in the Soviet ballet school.

Sakharov and Zeldovich took the view that training of talented youngsters in the fields of mathematics and physics should be accelerated rather than interrupted; there should be special programs in Soviet schools that would send these pupils into the universities and institutes at the age of sixteen or seventeen, two years earlier than normal and without any factory or farm work.

Their argument was that the most productive years in pure science were those of extreme youth; the ages of twenty-two to twenty-six were probably the most creative; and every effort should be made to equip the talented student to utilize the full powers of his intellect in this "golden interlude."

Sakharov and Zeldovich proposed a thorough shaking up of mathematics instruction, the abandonment of teaching of Euclidian geometry, less emphasis on algebraic problems and trigonometry, and concentration on probability theory, analytic geometry, calculus, and vector analysis. Their appeal won the day and special treatment of mathematics-physics students was decreed.

The more Sakharov began to think about social problems and particularly the social results of his work in the field of nuclear weaponry, the more concerned he became. As he was later to tell Hedrick Smith, the *New York Times* correspondent in Moscow:

"I gradually began to understand the criminal nature not only of nuclear tests but of the enterprise as a whole. I began to look on it and other world problems from a broader, human perspective."

It was the emergence of this philosophy that slowly but surely brought Sakharov into conflict with his government. He again unsuccessfully challenged Khrushchev, in September 1961, on the necessity of a series of large-scale nuclear tests. But he did not give up. He complained violently in 1962 about a third test series, which was held despite his objections.

"I could not," he told Hedrick Smith, "stop something I knew was wrong and unnecessary. It was terrible. I had an awful sense of powerlessness. After that I was a different man. I broke with my surroundings. It was a basic break."

Sakharov shifted his attention to the broader world of science and again he took the road of public protest. Soviet genetics, biology, botany, and agronomy had for years been poisoned by the dictatorship of a charlatan named Trofim D. Lysenko, who had won Stalin's confidence. Lysenko had employed his privileged position to destroy the foundations of Soviet genetics. He hounded the principal Soviet geneticist, N. I. Vavilov, into prison and death, drove many distinguished scientists from their posts, closed down some Soviet scientific institutes, and prostituted others to his own purposes. With Stalin's death Lysenko suffered a setback, but in the early 1960's he made a brief comeback under Khrushchev's auspices.

Sakharov joined forces with two Soviet agricultural specialists, V. P. Efroimson and F. D. Shchepotyev, to attack the persistence of Lysenkoism and to blame it for a criminal lag in Soviet genetics and biological theory. Although the president of the Soviet Agricultural Academy angrily rebuked Sakharov, the criticism struck home. Lysenko's comeback was halted and the Soviet government gave to biology and the life sciences the freedom from doctrinaire political interference that had already been won by the physical sciences.

When one of Lysenko's close associates, Nikolai Nuzhdin, was nominated for membership in the Academy of Sciences, Sakharov joined with many other Academicians in opposing Nuzhdin's candidacy, and it was rejected. Later, Sakharov was active in opposing Academic status for another Party hack, an agricultural propagandist named S. P. Trapeznikov. Khrushchev was incensed at Sakharov's interference in agricultural policy and, according to rumor, told the secret police to "teach Sakharov a lesson." When Khrushchev himself fell from power the move was dropped.

Sakharov knew that others within the scientific and political milieu felt much as he did about the issues with which he was concerned, and he was heartened when the United States and the Soviet Union agreed in 1963 to halt tests in the atmosphere, space, and under water. In fact, he took some credit for this agreement, because he called the attention of Yefim Slavsky, the minister of Medium Machine Building, to the American fall-back position, which President Eisenhower had put forward in 1959 calling for such a ban. The Russian side picked up this idea and the 1963 agreement was achieved.

Sakharov paid a price, however, for his growing political activity. He was dropped a couple of notches in his scientific status and this modified the high-security classification under which he had lived since 1950. But he was able to meet more freely with other Soviet members of the intelligentsia (it was in this period that he first became acquainted with Alexander Solzhenitsyn), and he began to publish once again in scientific journals. Two articles appeared in 1965, two more in 1966, and two in 1967. Moreover, the subjects of his scientific contributions revealed that he was turning from nuclear physics to much broader fields. He was writing about such questions as the quark phenomenon and the ever-expanding universe. From the sub-micro world of the atom he had moved to the macro-world of infinite space.

It is doubtful whether Sakharov envisaged at this point where his broadening exploration of the society in which he lived would lead him. But now, residing in Moscow instead of the cloistered nuclear community in Turkmenia, Sakharov was exchanging ideas with other scientists and a broadening circle of intellectuals, each of whom felt, in one way or another, that basic changes had to be made if the Soviet system was not to sink back into the terror-haunted morass into which Stalin had led it. This conviction found expression in a petition to the Communist Party leadership just before the Twenty-third Party Congress in 1966 in which Sakharov and twenty-four others, including Tamm, Kapitsa, the liberal writers Konstantin G. Paustovsky and Viktor Nekrasov, the ballerina Maya Plisetskaya, the movie director Mikhail I. Romm, and the grand old man of Soviet diplomacy, Ivan M. Maisky, called on the Party not to rehabilitate Stalin. That, they said, "would be a great disaster."

Whether their argument was compelling, whether in fact the Party leadership had planned to put Stalin back on the pedestal, is not known. But he was not rehabilitated and the decisions of the Twenty-second Party Congress condemning him were left on the books unchanged.

By this time certain hypotheses about his own society and about the world had begun to form in Sakharov's mind and, in his careful scientific manner, he started to test out his ideas. He circulated his theses among his friends both in the scientific community and in the new world of dissenting intellectuals. These were the basic ideas that comprised his famous Manifesto—*Progress, Coexistence, and Intellectual Freedom.*

The manifesto bears the date of June 1968. This was to prove a high watermark in the movement for liberalization within the Communist world. Sakharov's views found a ready reception and warm support in many layers of the Soviet intelligentsia and, even, it was whispered, in certain circles high within the government itself. They were widely circulated in *samizdat,* the typewritten self-publication process, which swiftly carried his views to almost every larger community within the Soviet Union. Not that there was unanimity over Sakharov's opinions. The hallmark of the Russian *intelligent* is dispute, challenge, disagreement, and individuality. But the thinking of many was moving in the same direction as that of Sakharov.

What was that direction? His manifesto speaks for itself, but perhaps the tendency may be summed up as calling for genuine coexistence and cooperation on world problems by the United States and the Soviet Union; a belief in the general trend of the two systems to converge; a call for the end of the arms race and a concentration of Soviet-American resources to meet the world's critical problems, which he postulated as hunger and the uneven development of societies, racism, militarism, the wastage of resources.

In order for the Soviet Union to move forward Sakharov believed it had to liberalize internally, opening up conditions for freedom of thought and access to information, ending the censorship, ending all violations of human rights, ending the system of political prisoners, political trials, and political prisons; complete the de-Stalinization process; restrict the influence of neo-Stalinists; and carry out a general reform of the Soviet economic system.

Sakharov emphasized the tentativeness of many of his conclusions and called for frank, open discussion of his ideas with full publicity—not only within the Soviet Union but also throughout the world.

This discussion did not occur. Sakharov's manifesto was published in the United States, western Europe, and ultimately in almost all the world—except the Communist nations. It evoked intense interest in the United States. In many universities small Sakharov groups were formed, often with physicists as their nuclei, hoping to collaborate with Russian colleagues toward Sakharov's goals. But the manifesto was circulated in Russia only by underground means, and it was not discussed publicly except in polemical terms that distorted and concealed the nature of Sakharov's thinking.

The brutal suppression of the Czech government, and the proclamation of the "Brezhnev doctrine," which sought to justify Soviet armed intervention in any Communist country if there was a putative threat to what Moscow defined as the stability of the Communist world, closed off any hope that Sakharov's ideas would be permitted intelligent consideration within the Soviet Union.

The new atmosphere was quickly reflected in Sakharov's own life. He was discharged from the nuclear weapons program in an action taken with typical Soviet brutality. One morning he arrived at the laboratory as usual in his chauffeur-driven car (which he still has, one of the perquisites of being an Academician). But when he approached the working area the guard refused to admit him, saying that his security clearance had been withdrawn. Somewhat later he was told that he no longer had a job. It was nearly a year later that, apparently in embarrassment, Soviet authorities gave him a small position in the Lebedev Institute (where he had started his career) as a senior researcher, the lowest status in which one of his rank as Academician is permitted to be employed.

The new atmosphere found reflection in Sakharov's own conduct. More and more often he signed his name to petitions for intellectuals who had fallen into the hands of the secret police. He began to appear at the trials of writers and poets. When, as often happened, he was not permitted to enter the courtroom, he stood vigil outside in sub-zero temperatures with the handful of other Soviet dissidents who possessed the bravery, the fortitude, and the conviction to stand for hours under the harassment, sometimes physical, of Soviet police and plainclothes thugs.

Sakharov's wife died at this time, and a year later he remarried. He met his second wife on one of the protest vigils. She is Yelena Bonner, half-Armenian, half-Jewish (one of the slanders Soviet propagandists spew against Sakharov is that he is really a Jew named Sugar-

man), the daughter of a woman who spent sixteen years
in Stalinist prison camps and aunt of Eduard Kuznetsov,
who received a fifteen-year sentence in the Leningrad
hijacking trial.

Exposed to the half-world of Soviet dissidence, Sakharov's views steadily evolved. He directed the force of
his analytic powers more and more not at the secrets of
atomic nuclei but at the complex and contradictory aspects of Soviet life.

Early in 1970, recognizing that some of the precepts
of his manifesto had been overrun by events and also because his own thinking was in a steady process of evolution, Sakharov issued a second programmatic document,
this one signed not only by himself but also by the physicist Valentin F. Turchin and the historian Roy A. Medvedev.

The new document, sometimes referred to as Manifesto II, had a different thrust from the first. It was
couched in the form of a letter to the Soviet leadership
—Leonid I. Brezhnev, Aleksei N. Kosygin, and Nikolai
V. Podgorny—and predominantly addressed itself to the
major internal problems of the Soviet Union: the slowing
down of the economy, Soviet failure to meet the challenge
of the computer world, which Sakharov described as "the
second industrial revolution," the increasing need for free
exchange of information and thought, the stultifying
bureaucracy, the adventurous nature of Soviet foreign
policy, especially in the Middle East, and the possibility
that unless the course was swiftly changed, the Soviet
Union would sink rapidly to the status of second-rate
power.

"There is no way out of the difficulties facing the

country," Sakharov and his colleagues declared, "except a course toward democratization carried out by the Party in accordance with a carefully worked out program."

This document was forwarded to the Soviet leadership in March 1970 but evoked no response.

Convinced that the core of the problem lay in the consistent, tenacious refusal of the Soviet leadership to grant its people normal freedoms of thought, of speech, of inquiry, of assemblage, of philosophical speculation, of a principled rule of law, Sakharov in 1970 took the remarkable step of forming with two young physicist friends what they called the Committee on Human Rights. The Committee, in its founding declaration signed by Sakharov, A. N. Tverdokhlebov and V. N. Chalidze, November 4, 1970, declared its intent to work within the framework of Soviet law to assist in creating and implementing guarantees of human rights based upon the humanitarian principles of the Universal Declaration of Human Rights adopted by the United Nations in 1948. The Committee proposed to assist persons concerned with the research and study of human rights in a socialist society, to carry on legal education in this field, and to engage in "constructive criticism of the contemporary state of the system of legal guarantees of individual liberty in Soviet law."

Both Tverdokhlebov and Chalidze promptly lost their positions as a result of their membership in the Committee. Chalidze was finally permitted to come to the United States in 1972 with his wife to deliver a series of lectures. Shortly after his arrival two Soviet officials obtained his passport under false pretenses in the lobby of the hotel where he was staying and immediately declared he had been deprived of Soviet citizenship. (A similar trick was played in London on Zhores Medvedev, brother of Roy A. Medvedev, who was associated with Sakharov in signing the 1970 manifesto. Zhores, a biologist, had been briefly confined to a Soviet mental institution as part of the Soviet campaign of repression of intellectuals. He was freed after protests from his brother, Sakharov, Solzhenitsyn, and others. He was then permitted to go to London to engage in scientific work and there, as in the case of Chalidze, a Soviet official persuaded him to hand over his passport and then promptly declared that he had been deprived of citizenship.)

Under the impact of these events Sakharov's scientific career came to a virtual standstill. Through 1973 he continued to go to the Lebedev Institute once a week to participate in a seminar on quantum theory, but he told friends that under the circumstances of his life he was unable to do any really fruitful work. In fact, he expressed concern whether at his age and after such a long interlude he would be able to make any further major contributions to physical theory.

He faced other unpleasantness. The three children of his first marriage, two married daughters and a sixteen-year-old son, began to shun him. The son went to live with his eldest daughter. His stepdaughter, who was studying in Moscow University's journalism school, was dismissed. Her husband, an engineer, lost his job. A sixteen-year-old stepson was barred from Moscow University, his examination papers deliberately tampered with by authorities. Later, the boy was admitted to the Lenin Pedagogical Institute.

None of these discouragements swayed Sakharov from what had become the central purpose of his life—the struggle for the renaissance of Soviet society and the liberation of the system from the repressive framework that he was convinced would produce nothing but disaster.

On March 5, 1971, the eighteenth anniversary of Stalin's death and three years after composing his original manifesto, Sakharov again addressed himself to Party Secretary Brezhnev. Recalling his 1968 Declaration and the letter of 1970 signed by himself, Medvedev, and Turchin, he submitted a new document further refining his views on the critical issues confronting the Soviet Union. He enclosed for Brezhnev's information some basic documentation on the Committee on Human Rights.

Sakharov's goals were unchanged. Once again, he called for a general liberalization, an end to the political prison system, an end to the use of psychiatric institutions to punish sane prisoners, full legal rights for all Soviet citizens, an end to repressions on political, ideological, and religious grounds, freedom of information and press, full restoration of the rights of all nationalities and individuals repressed by Stalin, a rule of law, an end to dogmatism, adventurism, and aggression. He called for basic economic reform, democratic elections, efforts to modernize agriculture, a radical improvement in the educational system, a full-scale anti-pollution and environmental program.

Sakharov had less to say on international relations, but he called for an international conference on the problems of peace, disarmament, economic aid to backward countries, defense of human rights, and protection of the environment. He agreed with the Kremlin that the principal threat to Russia came from China.

Once again, there was no response from Brezhnev.

A year later, in June 1972, he addressed to Brezhnev a fourth memorandum, a postscript to that of March 5, 1971, in which he urged "the democratization of society, the development of openness in public affairs, the rule of law and the safeguarding of basic human rights." These he deemed to be of decisive importance. He sharply criticized Soviet "apathy, hypocrisy, petit bourgeois egoism and hidden cruelty," the secret privileges of the elite, their indifference to human rights, progress, genuine security, and the future of mankind.

"The country's spiritual regeneration," he declared, "demands the elimination of those conditions that drive people into becoming hypocritical and time-serving, and that lead to feelings of impotence, discontent, and disillusionment."

He struck again at the failing Soviet standards of education and public health and expressed alarm at the rising wave of political arrests and repressions.

This time he concentrated almost exclusively on domestic Soviet concerns except for a passing reference to the Soviet industrial-military complex, which, he said, played a role analogous to that of the United States in foreign relations.

By this time the growing police repression against intellectuals had severely reduced Sakharov's circle of friends and associates and had begun to limit his influence within the intelligentsia, and more Soviet citizens began to perceive the potential danger of association with or contact with Sakharov.

The year 1973 was marked by constantly rising struggle. Soviet authorities brought their campaign against Sakharov into the open. Polemic attacks and increased police surveillance became common. Sakharov was called in by Mikhail P. Malyarov, first deputy Prosecutor General, the number two Soviet law enforcement officer, and warned that his conduct was under the strictest government scrutiny. Malyarov hinted that Sakharov might be prosecuted for violation of the Soviet state secrets act.

Simultaneously, a storm was whipped up against Sakharov in the Party press. Party speakers denounced him in their agitational meetings. The stage, it appeared, was being set for the public trial and conviction of Sakharov and his sentencing to the Soviet prison camp system, against which he had so long campaigned.

Then came a sudden turn. Sakharov, mild of manner, shy of appearance, began to fight back. He granted a series of interviews, including a notable discussion over Swedish radio in which he laid his case before world public opinion. He revealed his growing disenchantment with the Soviet system and his increasing doubt that it could, in fact, be regenerated from within. He was, he explained, not a Communist himself. "Philosophically, I am a liberal and a humanist," he said. The Soviet Union, he felt, had drifted away from Marxism and now was marked by intolerance, great-power chauvinism, hypocrisy, brutality, illegality, egoism, and conformism. He saw it as a pragmatic state not a doctrinal one, and he found himself growing more and more skeptical of socialism as a theory. He found less and less in its ability to solve in some special way the great problems of the world. States with socialist systems, he believed, tended to have the same kinds of problems as capitalist states. And the Soviet Union, he believed, was distinguished among all states for the "maximum lack of freedom, maximum ideological rigidity and maximum pretentions about being the best society although it certainly is not that."

Sakharov's thinking in the years of his political awareness has been characterized by deep, continuous development. When he began to move out of the sheltered world of nuclear physics, his first interest lay in the societal problems arising from the development of nuclear weapons. In this his course was clearly comparable to that of Oppenheimer; both felt a rising concern over the implications of a nuclearized world and of the specific consequences of nuclear weapons—fallout, the arms race, the employment of super-weapons for international blackmail. At the same time Sakharov began to turn to other problems of the society in which he lived—problems of education, of scientific development, of professional charlatanism. The deeper he moved into these questions the more his political consciousness expanded. And, much as Oppenheimer had, he began to be concerned with the issues underlying the arms race and the necessity for international collaboration in place of competition and conflict.

The Sakharov manifesto entitled *Progress, Coexistence, and Intellectual Freedom* was permeated with a humanitarian internationalist approach. He believed strongly in the possibility of parallel or converging paths for the Soviet Union and the United States. The heart of his proposal was a joint US–USSR program devised, in essence, to save the world. His domestic program—his concern with civil rights, the liberalization of Soviet society, and the end of repression—was subordinated to internationalist ideals.

With the passage of years Sakharov's emphasis steadily shifted. More and more he became concerned with the essential tyranny and banality of Soviet society and system until in the last of the four programmatic statements he focused almost entirely on Soviet life. He had become convinced that without internal change the great goals of international collaboration could not be achieved and, moreover, that the Soviet Union itself as a world power was headed toward decline and weakness because its technological-scientific intelligentsia was unable to keep the country competitively viable, especially with the United States, so long as it was subjected to the dull and dangerous dregs of the Stalinist terror system.

Throughout this period Sakharov shared Moscow's vision of Peking as the most dangerous enemy and, especially in his early writings, he merely repeated the standardized Soviet view of China as an aberrational power, unpredictable and maniacal. In fact, not until 1973 and rather late in that year did Sakharov frankly retract his early evaluations of China and express the belief that he had wrongly assessed the nature of the Sino-Soviet confrontation.

It is in the light of this evolution that Sakharov's important 1973 declaration on the Soviet-American détente must be understood. From the beginning of his consciousness of world politics he had been an advocate of détente, long before the Soviet government began to take this line and long before the Brezhnev-Nixon conversations brought it toward fulfillment.

Détente and collaboration between the Soviet Union and the United States were perceived by Sakharov as the core of a stable and secure world order. But with the passage of years it became more and more apparent to him that genuine détente could not be achieved when one partner was, in essence, only half free. Only if Russia resolved her internal contradictions, came to grips with the reality of the post-Stalin system of terror, with its police and the prison camps, only if the Soviet moved toward individual freedom, freedom of scientific inquiry, and public debate, and ended the sterility of the single-party system and the authoritarian imposition of the single Party line would the Soviet, in Sakharov's opinion, prove a reliable partner in a genuine détente.

Unless these internal problems were resolved, he was convinced, there was nothing to prevent a Soviet oligarchy from deceptively entering a pseudo-entente with the full intention of overturning it to its own advantage and thus, quite possibly, producing the destruction of the world.

It was this conviction, logically arrived at through the most systematic study, that led Sakharov to his fierce and open battle with the Soviet powers over the issue of liberalization of American trade with the Soviet Union and his opposition to close-knit economic and technological collaboration. He declared that the Soviet should not be given these advantages until or unless there was a reliable guarantee of internal Soviet liberalization.

As his struggle with Soviet authorities grew more intense, Sakharov received an invitation to come to Princeton University with his family for a year's study and lectures. Massachusetts Institute of Technology invited his stepdaughter, her husband, and his stepson to teach and study. Sakharov was reluctant to leave the Soviet Union, even if permission was granted, unless he could be assured of his return. The example of his friends

Chalidze and Medvedev, deprived of their passports and
citizenship, was vivid in his mind. There was also the
critical question of the Human Rights Movement in the
Soviet Union. Through police repression, arrest, intimida-
tion, and enforced deportation, few of the small band
remained active in Russia. Would the movement collapse
if Sakharov left, possibly never to return? This issue lay
at the heart of the dilemma Sakharov faced at New
Year's, 1974—a holiday he spent not in traditional cele-
bration, nowhere gayer than in Moscow, but in a hospital
with his wife, where both had gone for treatment of
serious physical ailments that had begun to sap their
strength. They had gone, as well, for a brief respite of
calm and comparative serenity in which to review the
state of the Soviet Union as it moved into its fifty-seventh
year of existence and what they might best do in accordance with the credo of the Russian *intelligent* of self-
sacrifice and dedication to the cause of the Russian
people.

                                                HARRISON E. SALISBURY

# INTRODUCTION

This collection contains the majority of my writings and statements on social, legal, and political subjects for the past several years. Some of them require elucidation, especially for the foreign reader. No doubt the best way to avoid possible misunderstandings would be to give an account, with a maximum of detail and frankness, of the internal and external circumstances that shaped my attitude and position. But at present I do not feel capable of doing this thoroughly, and shall confine myself to the necessary minimum. In giving autobiographical information, I am hoping to put an end to false rumors with respect to facts that have frequently been misrepresented in the press, owing to ignorance or sensationalism.

I was born in 1921 in Moscow, into a cultured and close family. My father was a teacher of physics and the author of several widely known textbooks and popular-science books. From childhood I lived in an atmosphere of decency, mutual help, and tact, a liking for work, and respect for the mastery of one's chosen profession. In 1938 I completed high school and entered Moscow State University, from which I was graduated in 1942. From 1942 to 1945 I worked as an engineer at a war plant, where I developed several inventions having to do with methods of quality control.

From 1945 to 1947 I did graduate work under the guidance of a well-known Soviet scientist, the theoretical physicist Igor Evgenevich Tamm. A few months after defending my dissertation for the degree of Candidate of Doctor of Science, roughly equivalent to an American Ph.D., which occurred in the spring of 1948, I was included in a research group working on the problem of a thermonuclear weapon. I had no doubts as to the vital importance of creating a Soviet super-weapon—for our country and for the balance of power throughout the world. Carried away by the immensity of the task, I worked very strenuously and became the author or co-author of several key ideas. In the Western press I have often been called "the father of the hydrogen bomb." This description reflects very inaccurately the real (and complex) situation of collective invention—something I shall not discuss in detail.

In the summer of 1950, almost simultaneously with the beginning of work on the thermonuclear weapon, I. E. Tamm and I began work on the problem of a controlled thermonuclear reaction; i.e., on the utilization of the nuclear energy of light elements for purposes of industrial power. In 1950 we formulated the idea of the magnetic thermo-isolation of high-temperature plasma,

and completed estimates on the parameters for thermonuclear synthesis installations. This research, which became known abroad through a paper read by I. V. Kurchatov at Harwell in 1956 and through the materials of
the First Geneva Conference on the Peaceful Use of
Atomic Energy, was recognized as pioneering. In 1961 I
proposed, for the same purposes, the heating of deuterium
with a beam from a pulse laser. I mention these things
here by way of explaining that my contributions were not
limited to military problems.

In 1950 our research group became part of a special
institute. For the next eighteen years I found myself
caught up in the routine of a special world of military
designers and inventors, special institutes, committees
and learned councils, pilot plants and proving grounds.
Every day I saw the huge material, intellectual, and nervous resources of thousands of people being poured into
the creation of a means of total destruction, something
potentially capable of annihilating all human civilization.
I noticed that the control levers were in the hands of
people who, though talented in their own way, were cynical. Until the summer of 1953 the chief of the atomic
project was Beria, who ruled over millions of slave-prison-
ers. Almost all the construction was done with their
labor. Beginning in the late fifties, one got an increasingly
clearer picture of the collective might of the military-industrial complex and of its vigorous, unprincipled leaders,
blind to everything except their "job." I was in a rather
special position. As a theoretical scientist and inventor,
relatively young and (moreover) not a Party member,
I was not involved in administrative responsibility and
was exempt from Party ideological discipline. My position

enabled me to know and see a great deal. It compelled
me to feel my own responsibility; and at the same time
I could look upon this whole perverted system as something of an outsider. All this prompted me—especially in
the ideological atmosphere that came into being after the
death of Stalin and the Twentieth Congress of the CPSU
—to reflect in general terms on the problems of peace and
mankind, and in particular on the problems of a thermonuclear war and its aftermath.

Beginning in 1957 (not without the influence of statements on this subject made throughout the world by such
people as Albert Schweitzer, Linus Pauling, and others) I
felt myself responsible for the problem of radioactive contamination from nuclear explosions. As is known, the ab-
sorption of the radioactive products of nuclear explosions
by the billions of people inhabiting the earth leads to an
increase in the incidence of several diseases and birth defects, of so-called sub-threshold biological effects—for example, because of damage to DNA molecules, the bearers
of heredity. When the radioactive products of an explosion
get into the atmosphere, each megaton of the nuclear explosion means thousands of unknown victims. And each
series of tests of a nuclear weapon (whether they be conducted by the United States, the USSR, Great Britain,
China, or France) involves tens of megatons; i.e., tens of
thousands of victims.

In my attempts to explain this problem, I encountered great difficulties—and a reluctance to understand. I
wrote memorandums (as a result of one of them I. V.
Kurchatov made a trip to Yalta to meet with Khrushchev
in an unsuccessful attempt to stop the 1958 tests), and I
spoke at conferences. I remember that in the summer of

1961 there was a meeting between atomic scientists and the chairman of the Council of Ministers, Khrushchev. It turned out that we were to prepare for a series of tests that would bolster up the new policy of the USSR on the German question (the Berlin Wall). I wrote a note to Khrushchev, saying: "To resume tests after a three-year moratorium would undermine the talks on banning tests and on disarmament, and would lead to a new round in the armaments race—especially in the sphere of intercontinental missiles and anti-missile defense." I passed it up the line. Khrushchev put the note in his breast pocket and invited all present to dine. At the dinner table he made an off-the-cuff speech that I remember for its frankness, and that did not reflect merely his personal position. He said more or less the following: Sakharov is a good scientist. But leave it to us, who are specialists in this tricky business, to make foreign policy. Only force—only the disorientation of the enemy. We can't say aloud that we are carrying out our policy from a position of strength, but that's the way it must be. I would be a slob, and not chairman of the Council of Ministers, if I listened to the likes of Sakharov. In 1960 we helped to elect Kennedy with our policy. But we don't give a damn about Kennedy if he is tied hand and foot—if he can be overthrown at any moment.

Another and no less dramatic episode occurred in 1962. The Ministry, acting basically from bureaucratic interests, issued instructions to proceed with a routine test explosion that was actually useless from the technical point of view. The explosion was to be powerful, so that the number of anticipated victims was colossal. Realizing the unjustifiable, criminal nature of this plan, I made desperate efforts to stop it. This went on for several weeks—

weeks that, for me, were full of tension. On the eve of the test I phoned the minister and threatened to resign. The minister replied: "We're not holding you by the throat." I was able to put a phone call through to Ashkabad, where Khrushchev was stopping on that particular day, and begged him to intervene. The next day I had a talk with one of Khrushchev's close advisers. But by then the time for the test had already been moved up to an earlier hour, and the carrier aircraft had already transported its burden to the designated point for the explosion. The feeling of impotence and fright that seized me on that day has remained in my memory ever since, and it has worked much change in me as I moved toward my present attitude.

In 1962 I visited the minister of the atomic industry, who at that time was in a suburban government sanatorium together with the deputy minister of foreign affairs, and presented an important idea that had been brought to my attention by one of my friends. By then, talks on the banning of nuclear testing had already been going on for several years, the stumbling block being the difficulty of monitoring underground explosions. But radioactive contamination is caused only by explosions in the atmosphere, in space, and in the ocean. Therefore, limiting the agreement to banning tests in these three environments would solve both problems (contamination and monitoring). It should be noted that a similar proposal had previously been made by President Eisenhower, but at the time it had not accorded with the thinking of the Soviet side. In 1963 the so-called Moscow Treaty, in which this idea was realized, was concluded on the initiative of Khrushchev and Kennedy. It is possible that my initiative was of help in this historic act.

In 1964 I spoke at a conference of the Academy of Sciences USSR (in connection with the election of one of Lysenko's companions-in-arms) and publicly touched on the "prohibited" subject of the situation in Soviet biology in which, for decades, modern genetics had been attacked as a "pseudo-science" and scientists working in that field had been subjected to harsh persecution and repression. Subsequently I developed these thoughts in greater detail in a letter to Khrushchev. Both the speech and the letter found a very broad response, and later helped to correct the situation to some extent. It was at this time that my name first appeared in the Soviet press—in an article by the president of the Academy of Agricultural Sciences that contained the most unpardonable attacks on me.

For me, personally, these events had great psychological significance. Furthermore, they expanded the circle of persons with whom I associated. In particular, I became acquainted during the next few years with the Medvedev brothers, Zhores and Roy. A manuscript by the biologist Zhores Medvedev, which was passed from hand to hand, circumventing the censor, was the first *samizdat* work I had read. (*Samizdat* was a word that had come into use a few years before to denote a new social phenomenon.) In 1967 I also read the manuscript of a book by the historian Roy Medvedev on the crimes of Stalin. Both books, and especially the latter, made a very strong impression on me. However our relations may have turned out, and whatever my subsequent disagreements with the Medvedevs on matters of principle, I cannot minimize their role in my own development.

In 1966 I was one of the signers of a collective letter on the "cult" of Stalin sent to the Twenty-third Congress

of the CPSU. In that same year I sent a telegram to the
Supreme Soviet of the USSR about a new law, then being
drafted, which would facilitate large-scale persecutions
for one's convictions (Article 190–1 of the RSFSR Criminal Code). Thus, for the first time my own fate became
intertwined with the fate of that group of people—a group
that was small but very weighty on the moral (and, I dare
say, the historical) plane—who subsequently came to be
called "dissenters" (*inakomyslyashchie*). (Personally, I
am fonder of the old Russian word "freethinkers"—
*volnomyslyashchie*.) Very shortly thereafter I had occasion to write a letter to Brezhnev protesting the arrest of
four of them: A. Ginzburg, Yu. Galanskov (who perished
tragically in a camp in 1972), V. Lashkova, and Dobrovolsky. In connection with this letter and my previous
actions, the minister heading up the department for which
I worked said of me: Sakharov is an outstanding scientist
and we have rewarded him well, but he is "stupid as a
politician."

In 1967, for a publication that circulated among my
colleagues, I wrote a "futurological" article on the future
role of science in the life of society, and on the future of
science itself. In that same year, for the *Literaturnaya
Gazeta*, the journalist E. Henry (Genri) and I wrote an
article on the role of the intelligentsia and the danger of
a thermonuclear war. The Central Committee of the
CPSU did not authorize publication of the article. But by
means unknown to me it got into the *Political Diary*—a
supposedly secret publication, something like *samizdat*
for higher officials. A year later both of these articles,
which remained little known, served as the basis for a
work destined to play a central role in my activity for

social causes. Early in 1968 I began work on a book I called *Progress, Coexistence, and Intellectual Freedom.* I wanted that book to reflect my thoughts on the most important problems facing mankind: thoughts on war and peace, on dictatorship, on the prohibited subject of Stalinist terror and freedom of thought, on demographic problems and the pollution of the environment, on the role that can be played by science and technological progress. The general tenor of the book was affected by the time of its writing—the height of the "Prague Spring." The basic ideas I tried to develop in the book were neither very new nor original. Essentially it was a compilation of liberal, humanistic, and "scientocratic" ideas based on information available to me and on personal experience. Today I regard this work as eclectic, pretentious in places, and imperfect ("raw") in terms of form. Nonetheless its basic ideas are dear to me. In it I clearly formulated the thesis (which strikes me as very important) that the rapprochement of the socialist and capitalist systems, accompanied by democratization, demilitarization, and social and technological progress, is the only alternative to the ruin of mankind. Beginning in May and June of 1968, *Progress* was widely distributed in the USSR. This was the first work of mine that was taken up by *samizdat.* In July and August came the first foreign reports of my book. Subsequently it was published abroad in large printings and provoked a great flow of responses in the press of many countries. In addition to the content of the work, an important role in all this was undoubtedly played by the fact that it was one of the first sociopolitical works to reach the West and that, moreover, its author was a highly decorated representative of the "secret" and "dread" specialty of nuclear physics. (Unfortunately, this sensationalism still envelops me, especially on the pages of the mass press in the West.)

The publication of this volume abroad immediately resulted in my being taken off secret projects (in August of 1968), and in the restructuring of my entire way of life. It was precisely at that time that I, acting under the influence of impulses I now consider unsound, transferred almost all my savings to a government fund (for the construction of a hospital for cancer patients), and to the Red Cross. At that time I had no personal contacts with people in need of help. Today, constantly seeing around me people who need not only protection but also material help, I often regret my overly hasty gesture.

In 1969 I was sent to work at the Physics Institute of the Academy of Sciences USSR, where I had once done graduate work and then been a collaborator of Igor Evgenevich Tamm. Although this meant a substantial drop in salary and job status, I was still able to continue scientific work in that area of physics most interesting to me: the theory of elementary particles. Unfortunately, however, in recent years I have not been satisfied with my productivity in scientific work. Two things have played a decisive role in this: first, the fact that, as theoretical physicists go, I am well along in years; second, the stressful—and recently very alarming—situation in which people close to me, my family, and I have found ourselves.

Meantime, events in society and an inner need to oppose injustice continued to urge me toward new actions. Early in 1970 another open letter to the leaders of the state was published by Valentin Turchin (the physicist and mathematician), Roy Medvedev, and myself. The subject of the letter was the interdependence of the problems of democratization and techno-economic progress. In June I took an active part in the campaign to free the other Medvedev brother—the biologist Zhores—from illegal confinement in a psychiatric hospital. About that same time I joined in a collective supervisory protest* to the Prosecutor's Office of the USSR on the case of General P. G. Grigorenko, who by decision of a Tashkent court had been sent for compulsory treatment to a special prison-type hospital of the MVD** in the town of Chernyakhovsk. The reason for this was the fact that Grigorenko had repeatedly made public appeals in defense of political prisoners and in defense of the rights of the Crimean Tatars, who in 1944 had been resettled from the Crimea with great cruelties under the Stalinist tyranny, and who today cannot return to their homeland. Our appeal, which pointed out the many patent violations of the law in the Grigorenko case, was never answered (which is also a crude violation of the law). Thus even more closely than in 1968, I was brought into contact with what is perhaps one of the most shameful aspects of present-day Soviet reality: illegality, and the cynical persecution of persons coming out in defense of basic human rights. But at the same time I got to know several of these persons, and subsequently many others. One of those who joined in the collective protest on the Grigorenko case was Valery Chalidze, with whom I became very close.

* I.e., a protest demanding that the Prosecutor's office intervene (as it is entitled to do under Soviet law) to order review of a case "by way of supervision." [Translator's note.]

** Ministry of Internal Affairs. [Translator's note.]

I became even more familiar with the problems of defending human rights in October 1970, when I was allowed to attend a political trial. The mathematician Revolt Pimenov and the puppet-show actor Boris Vail had been charged with distributing *samizdat*—giving friends books and manuscripts to read. The items named in their case included an article by Djilas, the Czech manifesto "Two Thousand Words," Pimenov's personal commentaries on Khrushchev's speech at the Twentieth Congress, etc. I sat in a courtroom filled with "probationers" of the KGB, while the friends of the defendants remained in a hallway on the ground floor throughout the trial. This is one more feature of all political trials, without exception. Formally, they are open. But the courtroom is packed in advance with KGB agents specially designated for the purpose, while another group of agents stands around the court on all sides. They are always in civilian clothes, they call themselves *druzhinniki*,* and they are allegedly preserving public order. This is the way it was (with negligible variations) in all cases when I was allowed to enter the courtroom. As for the passes enabling me to attend, they were apparently issued in acknowledgment of my previous services.

Pimenov and Vail were sentenced to five years of exile each, despite the fact that Vail's lawyer, at the appellate hearing, had argued convincingly that he had taken no part at all in the incidents incriminating him. In his concluding remarks Boris Vail said that an unjust sentence has an effect not only on the convicted person but also on the hearts of judges.

---

* I.e., members of a *druzhina,* or voluntary auxiliary police detachment. [Translator's note.]

From the autumn of 1971 on I was outside the line formed by the *druzhinniki*. But nothing else had changed. At the trial of the well-known astrophysicist Kronid Lyubarsky (who was charged with the same thing—distributing *samizdat*) a very significant and tragic show was put on. We were not allowed in the courtroom. And when the session began, the "unknown persons in civilian clothes" used force to push us out of the vestibule of the court into the street. Then a big padlock was hung on the door leading into the people's court. One has to see all these senseless and cruel dramatics with one's own eyes to feel it to the fullest. But why all this? The only answer I can give is that the farce being performed inside the courthouse is even less intended for public disclosure than the farce outside the courthouse. The bureaucratic logic of legal proceedings looks grotesque in the light of public disclosure, even when there is formal observance of the law—which is by no means always the case.

The sentence received by Pimenov and Vail, so harsh and unjust from the viewpoint of natural human norms, is relatively lenient compared to the decisions of Soviet courts in other cases of a similar nature, especially in recent years. Vladimir Bukovsky, known to the entire world for his protests in defense of people incarcerated in psychiatric hospitals for political reasons, was sentenced to twelve years: two years of prison, five years of camp, and five years of exile. K. Lyubarsky was sentenced to five years of imprisonment. The sentences passed outside of Moscow are even harsher. The young psychiatrist Semyon Gluzman was sentenced to seven years of imprisonment. I once happened to see Semyon for a few minutes at a railroad station, and I was astounded by the purity of his

countenance—by a kind of effective goodness and direct-
ness. At the time I had no way of suspecting that such a
fate was in store for him! It is generally supposed that
the reason for the reprisal against Gluzman was the as-
sumption that he was the author of "Expert Examination
*in Absentia* in the Grigorenko Case." But at the trial this
charge was not brought. V. Morozov and Yu. Shukhevich,
both authors of memoirs about their terms in camp, were
sentenced by a Ukrainian court to fourteen and fifteen
years, respectively, of imprisonment and exile. And the
number of similar reprisals has grown rapidly.

Before proceeding further, I should like to say a few
words as to why I attach so much importance to the
matter of defending political prisoners—defending the
freedom of one's convictions. In the course of fifty-six
years our country has undergone great shocks, sufferings,
and humiliations, the physical annihilation of millions of
the best people (best both morally and intellectually),
decades of official hypocrisy and demagoguery, of internal
and external time-serving. The era of terror—when tortures and special conferences[*] threatened everyone, when
they seized the most devoted servants of the regime
simply for the general count and to create an atmosphere
of fright and submission—is now behind us. But we are
still living in the spiritual atmosphere created by that
era. Against those few who do not go along with the
prevalent practices of compromise, the government uses
repression as before. Together with judicial repressions,
the most important and decisive role in maintaining this
atmosphere of internal and external submission is played

---

[*] Special conferences (or boards) was the designation given, in the Stalin
era, to secret drumhead courts, or troikas. [Translator's note.]

by the power of the state, which manipulates all economic and social control levers. This, more than anything else, keeps the body and soul of the majority of people in a state of dependence. Another major influence on the psychological situation in the country is the fact that people are weary of endless promises of economic flowering in the very near future, and have ceased altogether to believe in fine words. The standard of living (food, clothing, housing, possibilities for leisure), social conditions (children's facilities, medical and educational institutions, pensions, labor protection, etc.)—all these lag far behind the level in advanced countries. An indifference to social problems—an attitude of consumerism and selfishness—is developing among the broad strata of the population. And among the majority, protest against the deadening official ideology has an unconscious, latent character. The religious and national movements are the broadest and most conscious. Among those who fill the camps or are subjected to other persecutions are many believers and representatives of national minorities. One of the mass forms of protest is the desire to leave the country. Unfortunately, it must be noted that sometimes the striving toward a national revival takes on chauvinistic traits, and borders on the traditional "everyday" hostility toward "aliens." Russian anti-Semitism is an example of this. Thus a part of the Russian opposition intelligentsia is beginning to manifest a paradoxical closeness to the secret Party-state doctrine of nationalism, which in fact is increasingly replacing the anti-national and anti-religious myth of Bolshevism. Among some people the same feeling of dissatisfaction and internal protest takes on other asocial forms (drunkenness, crime).

It is very important that the facade of prosperity and enthusiasm not conceal from the world this real picture of things. Our experience must not come to nothing. And it is equally important that our society gradually emerge from the dead end of unspirituality, which closes off the possibilities not only for the development of spiritual culture but also for progress in the material sphere.

I am convinced that under the conditions obtaining in our country a position based on morality and law is the most correct one, as corresponding to the requirements and possibilities of society. What we need is the systematic defense of human rights and ideals and not a political struggle, which would inevitably incite people to violence, sectarianism, and frenzy. I am convinced that only in this way, provided there is the broadest possible public disclosure, will the West be able to recognize the nature of our society; and that then this struggle will become part of a worldwide movement for the salvation of all mankind. This belief constitutes a partial answer to the question as to why I have (naturally) turned from worldwide problems to the defense of individual people.

The position of those who, beginning with the trials of Sinyavsky and Daniel, Ginzburg and Galanskov, have struggled for justice as they understand it can probably be compared with the position of the world-famous apolitical organization "Amnesty International." In any democratic country the question of the legality of such activity could not even arise. In our country, unfortunately, such is not the case. Dozens of the most famous political trials and dozens of prisoners in psychiatric hospitals of the prison type provide a graphic demonstration of this.

In recent years I have learned a great deal about Soviet juridical practices, through attending trials and receiving information about the course of similar trials in other cities [besides Moscow]. I have also learned a great deal about conditions in places of confinement: about malnutrition, pitiless formalism, and repressions against prisoners. In several statements I called the attention of world public opinion to this problem, which is vitally important for the 1,700,000 Soviet prisoners and indirectly has a deep influence on many important aspects of the moral and social life of the whole country. I have appealed, and I again appeal, to all international organizations concerned with this problem—and especially to the International Red Cross—to abandon their policy of nonintervention in the internal affairs of the socialist countries as regards defending human rights and to manifest the utmost persistence. I have also spoken out on the institution of "conditional release with obligatory assignment to labor," which in a political sense represents a vestige of the Stalinist system of mass forced labor, and which is very frightening in a social sense. It is difficult even to imagine the nightmare of the barracks for the "conditionally released persons," with almost general drunkenness, fistfights, throat-slitting. This system has broken the lives of many people. The preservation of the camp system and forced labor is one of the reasons why extensive regions of the country are off-limits for foreigners. It would appear that the realization of any successful international cooperation in developing our very rich resources is impossible without the abolishment of this system.

Another problem that has claimed my attention in recent years is that of the psychiatric repressions used by organs of the KGB as an important auxiliary means of stifling and frightening dissenters. There is no doubt as to the tremendous social danger of this phenomenon.

The documents brought together in this collection reflect my striving to call attention to this set of problems.

I feel that I owe a debt too great to be repaid to the brave and good people who are incarcerated in prisons, camps, and psychiatric hospitals because they struggled to defend human rights.

◻

In the autumn of 1970, V. N. Chalidze, A. N. Tverdokhlebov, and I joined in founding the Human Rights Committee. This act on our part attracted great attention in the USSR and abroad. From the day of the Committee's founding, A. S. Volpin took an active part in its work. This was the first time that such an association had made its appearance in our country; and its members did not have a very precise idea of what they should do and how they should do it. Yet the Committee did a great deal of work on several problems, particularly in studying the question of compulsory confinement in psychiatric hospitals for political reasons. At the present time the work of the Committee is being carried on by I. R. Shafarevich, G. S. Podyapolsky, and myself. As was true of the "Initiative Group" created somewhat earlier, the very existence of the Committee, as a free group of associates independent of the authorities, has a unique and very great moral significance for our country.

◻

This collection includes a "Memorandum" written in the first months of 1971 and sent to L. I. Brezhnev in March of that year. In terms of form, the "Memorandum" is a kind of synopsis of an imaginary dialogue with the leadership of the country. I am not convinced that this form is literarily successful, but it is compact. As for the content, I endeavored to set forth my positive demands in the political, social, and economic spheres. Fifteen months later, not having received any reply, I published the "Memorandum," adding a "Postscript," which stands on its own. I call the reader's special attention to it.

In publishing the "Memorandum," I did not make any changes in the text. In particular, I did not change the treatment of the problem of Soviet-Chinese relations—something I now regret. I still do not idealize the Chinese variant of socialism. But I do not regard as correct the evaluation of the danger of Chinese aggression vis-à-vis the USSR that is given in the "Memorandum." In any case, the Chinese threat cannot serve as a justification for the militarization of our country and the absence of democratic reforms in it.

I have already said something about those documents in this collection that are associated with the defense of the rights of individual people. During the past few years I have learned of an increasingly large number of tragic and heroic fates, some of which are reflected in the pages of this collection. For the most part, the documents of this cycle require no commentary.

In April of 1972 I drew up the text of an appeal to the Supreme Soviet of the USSR to grant amnesty to political prisoners and abolish capital punishment. These documents were timed to coincide with the fiftieth anniversary of the USSR. I have already explained why I attribute such prime importance to the first of these questions. As for the latter, the abolishment of capital punishment is an extremely important act, both morally and socially, for any country. And in our country, with its very low level of legal consciousness and widespread animosity, this act would be especially important. I succeeded in gathering about fifty signatures for the appeals. Each of them represented a very ponderable moral and social act on the part of the signer. I felt this with particular force while I was gathering the signatures. Many more people refused than signed, and the explanations offered by some of them clarified for me much regarding the inner reasons for the thoughts and acts of our intelligentsia.

In September 1971 I sent a letter to the members of the Presidium of the Supreme Soviet of the USSR on freedom of emigration and unobstructed return. My letter to the U.S. Congress in September of 1973 was another *démarche* on this same subject. In these documents I call attention to various aspects of this problem, including the important role that its solution would play in the democratization of our country, and in raising its standard of living to the level of the advanced countries. The validity of this idea can be shown by the example of Poland and Hungary, where today freedom to leave the country and return to it is not so heavily encumbered as in our country.

In the summer of 1973 I was interviewed by Olle Stenholm, correspondent for a Swedish radio station, who asked me questions of a general character. This interview had a broad response in the USSR and foreign countries. I received several dozen letters expressing indignation at the "slanderous" line I had taken. (It should be borne in mind that letters of the opposite kind usually do not reach

me.) The Soviet *Literaturnaya Gazeta* published an article about me entitled "A Supplier of Slander." The correspondent who had interviewed me and published his
text without distortions was recently deprived of his entry
visa and the possibility of continuing his work in the
USSR. This was an outrageous violation of the rights of
an honest and intelligent journalist, who had become a
friend of my family. One cannot rule out the possibility
that the latter circumstance played its own role in the
illegality practiced upon him. The interview was verbal,
and neither questions nor answers were discussed in advance. This must be taken into account in evaluating the
document, which represents an unconstrained conversation, in a home setting, on very serious, basic problems.
In this interview, as in the "Memorandum" and the "Postscript," I went beyond the limits of the subject of the
rights of man and democratic freedoms and touched on
economic and social problems, which generally speaking
require special—and perhaps even professional—training.
But these problems are of such vital importance to every
person that I am not sorry they came up for discussion.
My opponents were especially irritated by my description
of our country's system as state capitalism with a Party-
state monopoly and the consequences, in all spheres of
social life, that flow from such a system.

Important basic problems of the "détente" in international tensions in their connection with a proviso for
the democratization and opening up of Soviet society
were reflected in the interview of August–September
1973.

In recent years I have carried on my activities under
conditions of ever-increasing pressure on me, and espe-

cially on my family. In September of 1972 our close friend
Yury Shikhanovich was arrested. In October of 1972
Tatyana, my wife's daughter, who was doing very well
in her studies, was expelled from the university in her last
year under a formal and far-fetched pretext. Throughout
the year we were harassed by anonymous telephone calls,
with threats and absurd accusations. In February of 1973
the *Literaturnaya Gazeta* published an article by its
editor-in-chief, Chakovsky, dealing with a book by Harrison Salisbury. In this article I was characterized as an
extremely naïve person who quoted the New Testament,
"coquettishly waved an olive branch," "played the holy
fool," and "willingly accepted the compliments of the
Pentagon." All this was said in connection with my
*Progress*, which thus, after five years, was mentioned
in the Soviet press for the first time. In March, likewise for
the first time, I was summoned to the KGB for a talk on
the pretext that my wife and I had jointly offered to go
surety for our friend Yury Shikhanovich. In June Tatyana's husband was deprived of work in connection with
having made an application to go and study in the United
States, pursuant to an invitation. In July the above-mentioned article, "A Supplier of Slander," appeared. Also in
July my wife's son Aleksei was refused admission to the
university, apparently on special orders from above. In
August I was summoned by the deputy prosecutor of the
USSR, Malyarov. The basic content of the talk was
threats. Then immediately after the interview of August
twenty-first on the problems of détente, Soviet newspapers reprinted items from foreign Communist papers
and a letter from forty Academicians declaring I was an
opponent of relaxation of international tensions. Next

came a nationwide newspaper campaign in which I was condemned by representatives of all strata of our society. In late September our apartment, thoroughly observed by the KGB, was visited by persons who called themselves members of the "Black September" organization. They threatened reprisals not only on me but also on the members of my family. In November an investigator who was a colonel in the KGB summoned my wife for repeated interrogations that lasted many hours. My wife refused to participate in the investigation, but this did not immediately put an end to the summonses. Previously she had publicly stated that she had sent to the West the diary of Eduard Kuznetsov, which had come into her hands. But she felt she was entitled not to tell what was done, or how it was done, by way of its distribution. The investigator warned her that her actions made her liable under Article 70 of the RSFSR Criminal Code, with a period of punishment of up to seven years. It seems to me this is quite enough for one family.

Soon after the coup d'état in Chile, the writers A. Galich and V. Maximov joined with me in an appeal to the new government expressing fears for the life of the outstanding Chilean poet Pablo Neruda. Our letter was not political in nature and had no other aims than strictly humane ones. But in the Soviet press and the pro-Soviet foreign press, it provoked an explosion of feigned indignation as allegedly "defending the fascist junta." Moreover, the letter itself was quoted inaccurately, and two of its authors—Galich and Maximov—were in general "forgotten." The aim of the organizers of this campaign—to compromise me at least in this way if it couldn't be done otherwise—was only too obvious.

But to digress from the subject of patently unscrupulous opponents and to turn to opinions that more objectively reflect liberal social opinion in the West, it must be said that this whole story brought to light a typical misunderstanding that merits discussion. As a rule, liberal social opinion in the democratic countries takes an international position, protesting against injustice and violence not only in one's own country but also throughout the world. It was not by accident that I said "as a rule." Unfortunately, it is very frequently the case that the defense of human rights in the socialist countries, by virtue of an opinion as to the special progressiveness of their regimes, falls outside (or almost falls outside) the field of activity of foreign organizations. The greater part of my efforts has been aimed precisely at changing this situation, which has been one of the reasons for our tragedies. However, that is not the point at issue here. Instead I should like to talk about that part of the Western liberal intelligentsia (still a small part) that extends its activities to the socialist countries as well. These people look to the Soviet dissenters for a reciprocal, analogous international position with respect to other countries. But there are several important circumstances they do not take into account: the lack of information; the fact that a Soviet dissenter is not only unable to go to other countries but also is deprived, within his own country, of the majority of sources of information; that the historical experience of our country has weaned us away from excessive "leftism," so that we evaluate many facts differently from the "leftist" intelligentsia of the West; that we must avoid political pronouncements in the international arena, where we are so ignorant (after all, we do not engage in political activity even in our own country); that we must avoid getting into the channel of Soviet propaganda, which so often deceives us. We know that in the Western countries there are vigilant and influential forces that protest (better and more effectively than we do) against injustice and violence there. We do not justify injustice or violence, wherever they appear. We do not feel that there is necessarily more in our country than in other countries. But at the moment our strength cannot suffice for the whole world. We ask that all this be taken into account, and that we be forgiven the errors we sometimes make in the dust kicked up by polemics.

The general position reflected in the materials of this collection is closer to my first book than might appear at first glance. [There are] differences in the treatment of political or politico-economic questions that are of course immediately apparent. But since I lay no claim to the role of discoverer or political adviser, these differences are less essential than the spirit of free debate and the concern for fundamental problems, which, I should like to think, are found both in *Progress* and in the recent writings.

The majority of my writings are either addressed to the leaders of our state or they have a specific foreign addressee. But inwardly I address them to all people on earth, and in particular to the people of my country, because they were dictated by concern and anxiety for my own country and its people.

I am not a purely negative critic of our way of life: I recognize much that is good in our people and in our country, which I ardently love. But I have been compelled to fix attention on negative phenomena, since they are precisely what the official propaganda passes over in silence, and since they represent the greatest damage and danger. I am not an opponent of détente, trade, or disarmament. On the contrary, in several writings I have called for just these things. It is precisely in convergence that I see the only way to the salvation of mankind. But I consider it my duty to point out all the hidden dangers of a false détente, a collusion-détente, or a capitulation-détente, and to call for utilization of the entire arsenal of means, of all efforts, to achieve real convergence, accompanied by democratization, demilitarization, and social progress. I hope that the publication of this collection will be of some use in that cause.

In conclusion, I should like to express my deep gratitude to all those who helped in the preparation and publishing of this collection: to the publisher, Mr. Knopf, to the editors, Messrs. Green and Salisbury, to my wife, and to my many friends in the USSR and other countries.

A. SAKHAROV

*December 31, 1973*
*Moscow*

# PROGRESS, COEXISTENCE, AND INTELLECTUAL FREEDOM

The views of the author were formed in the milieu of the scientific and scientific-technical intelligentsia, which manifests much anxiety over the principles and specific aspects of foreign and domestic policy and over the future of mankind. This anxiety is nourished, in particular, by a realization that the scientific method of directing policy, the economy, arts, education, and military affairs still has not become a reality.

We regard as "scientific" a method based on deep analysis of facts, theories, and views, presupposing un-prejudiced, unfearing open discussion and conclusions. The complexity and diversity of all the phenomena of modern life, the great possibilities and dangers linked with the scientific-technical revolution and with a number of social tendencies demand precisely such an approach, as has been acknowledged in a number of official statements.

In this essay, advanced for discussion, the author has set himself the goal to present, with the greatest conviction and frankness, two theses that are supported by many people in the world. The theses relate to the destruction threatened by the division of mankind and the need for intellectual freedom.

# I.

The division of mankind threatens it with destruction. Civilization is imperiled by: a universal thermonuclear war, catastrophic hunger for most of mankind, stupefaction from the narcotic of "mass culture," and bureaucratized dogmatism, a spreading of mass myths that put entire peoples and continents under the power of cruel and treacherous demagogues, and destruction or degeneration from the unforeseeable consequences of swift changes in the conditions of life on our planet.

In the face of these perils, any action increasing the division of mankind, any preaching of the incompatibility of world ideologies and nations is madness and a crime. Only universal cooperation under conditions of intellectual freedom and the lofty moral ideals of socialism and labor, accompanied by the elimination of dogmatism and pressures of the concealed interests of ruling classes, will preserve civilization.

The reader will understand that ideological collaboration cannot apply to those fanatical, sectarian, and extremist ideologies that reject all possibility of rapprochement, discussion, and compromise, for example, the ideologies of fascist, racist, militaristic, and Maoist demagogy.

Millions of people throughout the world are striving to put an end to poverty. They despise oppression, dogmatism, and demagogy (and their more extreme manifestations—racism, fascism, Stalinism, and Maoism). They believe in progress based on the use, under conditions of social justice and intellectual freedom, of all the positive experience accumulated by mankind.

# II.

The second basic thesis is that intellectual freedom is essential to human society—freedom to obtain and distribute information, freedom for open-minded and unfearing debate, and freedom from pressure by officialdom and prejudices. Such a trinity of freedom of thought is the only guarantee against an infection of people by mass myths, which, in the hands of treacherous hypocrites and demagogues, can be transformed into bloody dictatorship. Freedom of thought is the only guarantee of the feasibility of a scientific democratic approach to politics, economy, and culture.

But freedom of thought is under a triple threat in modern society—from the deliberate opium of mass culture, from cowardly, egotistic, and philistine ideologies, and from the ossified dogmatism of a bureaucratic oligarchy and its favorite weapon, ideological censorship. Therefore, freedom of thought requires the defense of all thinking and honest people. This is a mission not only for the intelligentsia but for all strata of society, particularly its most active and organized stratum, the working class. The worldwide dangers of war, famine, cults of personality, and bureaucracy—these are perils for all of mankind.

Recognition by the working class and the intelligentsia of their common interests has been a striking phenomenon of the present day. The most progressive, internationalist, and dedicated element of the intelligentsia is, in essence, part of the working class, and the most advanced, educated, internationalist, and broad-minded part of the working class is part of the intelligentsia.

This position of the intelligentsia in society renders senseless any loud demands that the intelligentsia subordinate its strivings to the will and interests of the working class (in the Soviet Union, Poland, and other socialist countries). What these demands really mean is subordination to the will of the Party or, even more specifically, to the Party's central apparatus and its officials. Who will guarantee that these officials always express the genuine interests of the working class as a whole and the genuine interests of progress rather than their own caste interests?

We will divide this essay into two parts. The first we will title "Dangers" and the second "The Basis of Hope." This essay contains much that is controversial and open to question; I invite response and debate.

# DANGERS

## THE THREAT OF NUCLEAR WAR

Three technical aspects of thermonuclear weapons have made thermonuclear war a peril to the very existence of humanity. These aspects are: the enormous destructive power of a thermonuclear explosion, the relative cheapness of rocket-thermonuclear weapons, and the practical impossibility of an effective defense against a massive rocket-nuclear attack.

□

Today one can consider a three-megaton nuclear warhead as "typical" (this is somewhere between the warhead of a Minuteman and of a Titan II). The area of fires from the explosion of such a warhead is 150 times greater than from the Hiroshima bomb, and the area of destruction is 30 times greater. The detonation of such a warhead over a city would create a 100-square-kilometer [40-square-mile] area of total destruction and fire.

Tens of millions of square meters of living space would be destroyed. No fewer than a million people would perish under the ruins of buildings, from fire and radiation, suffocating in the dust and smoke or dying in shelters buried under debris. In the event of a ground-level explosion, the fallout of radioactive dust would create a danger of fatal exposure in an area of tens of thousands of square kilometers.

□

A few words about the cost and the possible number of explosions.

After the stage of research and development has been passed, mass production of thermonuclear weapons and carrier rockets is no more complex and expensive than, for example, the production of military aircraft, which were produced by the tens of thousands during the war.

The annual production of plutonium in the world now is in the tens of thousands of tons. If one assumes that half this output goes for military purposes and that an average of several kilograms of plutonium goes into one warhead, then enough warheads have already been accumulated to destroy mankind many times over.

□

The third aspect of thermonuclear peril (along with the power and cheapness of warheads) is what we term the practical impossibility of preventing a massive rocket attack. This situation is well known to specialists. In the popular scientific literature, for example, one can read this in an article by Richard L. Garwin and Hans A. Bethe in the *Scientific American* of March 1968.

The technology and tactics of attack have now far surpassed the technology of defense despite the development of highly maneuverable and powerful anti-missiles with nuclear warheads and despite other technical ideas, such as the use of laser beams and so forth.

Improvements in the resistance of warheads to shock waves and to the radiation effects of neutron and X-ray exposure, the possibility of mass use of relatively light and inexpensive decoys that are virtually indistinguishable from warheads and exhaust the capabilities of an anti-missile defense system, a perfection of tactics of massed and concentrated attacks, in time and space, that overstrain the defense detection centers, the use of orbital and fractional-orbital attacks, the use of active and passive jamming, and other methods not disclosed in the press—all this has created technical and economic obstacles to an effective missile defense that, at the present time, are virtually insurmountable.

The experience of past wars shows that the first use of a new technical or tactical method of attack is usually highly effective even if a simple antidote can soon be developed. But in a thermonuclear war the first blow may be the decisive one and render null and void years of work and billions spent on creation of an anti-missile system.

An exception to this would be the case of a great technical and economic difference in the potentials of two enemies. In such a case, the stronger side, creating an anti-missile defense system with a multiple reserve, would face the temptation of ending the dangerous and unstable balance once and for all by embarking on a pre-emptive adventure, expending part of its attack potential on destruction of most of the enemy's launching bases and counting on impunity for the last stage of escalation, i.e., the destruction of the cities and industry of the enemy.

Fortunately for the stability of the world, the difference between the technical-economic potentials of the Soviet Union and the United States is not so great that one of the sides could undertake a "preventive aggression" without an almost inevitable risk of a destructive retaliatory blow. This situation would not be changed by a broadening of the arms race through the development of anti-missile defenses.

In the opinion of many people, an opinion shared by the author, a diplomatic formulation of this mutually comprehended situation, for example, in the form of a moratorium on the construction of anti-missile systems, would be a useful demonstration of a desire of the Soviet Union and the United States to preserve the status quo and not to widen the arms race for senselessly expensive anti-missile systems. It would be a demonstration of a desire to cooperate, not to fight.

A thermonuclear war cannot be considered a continuation of politics by other means (according to the formula of Clausewitz). It would be a means of universal suicide.

Two kinds of attempts are being made to portray thermonuclear war as an "ordinary" political act in the eyes of public opinion. One is the concept of the "paper tiger," the concept of the irresponsible Maoist adventurists. The other is the strategic doctrine of escalation, worked out by scientific and militarist circles in the United States. Without minimizing the seriousness of the challenge inherent in that doctrine, we will just note that the political strategy of peaceful coexistence is an effective counterweight to the doctrine.

A complete destruction of cities, industry, transport, and systems of education, a poisoning of fields, water, and air by radioactivity, a physical destruction of the larger part of mankind, poverty, barbarism, a return to savagery, and a genetic degeneracy of the survivors under the impact of radiation, a destruction of the material and information basis of civilization—this is a measure of the peril that threatens the world as a result of the estrangement of the world's two super-powers.

Every rational creature, finding itself on the brink of a disaster, first tries to get away from the brink and only then does it think about the satisfaction of its other needs. If mankind is to get away from the brink, it must overcome its divisions.

A vital step would be a review of the traditional method of international affairs, which may be termed "empirical-competitive." In the simplest definition, this is a method aiming at maximum improvement of one's position everywhere possible and, simultaneously, a method of causing maximum unpleasantness to opposing forces without consideration of common welfare and common interests.

If politics were a game of two gamblers, then this would be the only possible method. But where does such a method lead in the present unprecedented situation?

# VIETNAM AND THE MIDDLE EAST

In Vietnam, the forces of reaction, lacking hope for an expression of national will in their favor, are using the force of military pressure. They are violating all legal and moral norms and are carrying out flagrant crimes against humanity. An entire people is being sacrificed to the proclaimed goal of stopping the "Communist tide."

They strive to conceal from the American people considerations of personal and Party prestige, the cynicism and cruelty, the hopelessness and ineffectiveness of the anti-Communist tasks of American policy in Vietnam, as well as the harm this war is doing to the true goals of the American people, which coincide with the universal tasks of bolstering peaceful coexistence.

To end the war in Vietnam would first of all save the people perishing there. But it also is a matter of saving peace in all the world. Nothing undermines the possibilities of peaceful coexistence more than a continuation of the war in Vietnam.

Another tragic example is the Middle East. If direct responsibility for Vietnam rests with the United States, in the Middle East direct responsibility rests not with the United States but with the Soviet Union (and with Britain in 1948 and 1956).

On the one hand, there was an irresponsible encouragement of so-called Arab unity (which in no way had a socialist character—look at Jordan—but was purely nationalist and anti-Israel). It was said that the struggle of the Arabs had an essentially anti-imperialist character. On the other hand, there was an equally irresponsible encouragement of Israeli extremists.

We cannot here analyze the entire contradictory and tragic history of the events of the last twenty years, in the course of which the Arabs and Israel, along with historically justified actions, carried out reprehensible deeds, often brought about by the actions of external forces.

Thus, in 1948, Israel waged a defensive war. But in 1956, the actions of Israel appeared reprehensible. The preventive six-day war in the face of threats of destruction by merciless, numerically vastly superior forces of the Arab coalition could have been justifiable. But the cruelty to refugees and prisoners of war and the striving to settle territorial questions by military means must be condemned. Despite this condemnation, the breaking of relations with Israel appears a mistake, complicating a peaceful settlement in this region and complicating a necessary diplomatic recognition of Israel by the Arab governments.

In our opinion, certain changes must be made in the

conduct of international affairs, systematically subordinating all concrete aims and local tasks to the basic task of actively preventing an aggravation of the international situation, of actively pursuing and expanding peaceful coexistence to the level of cooperation, of making policy in such a way that its immediate and long-range effects will in no way sharpen international tensions and will not create difficulties for either side that would strengthen the forces of reaction, militarism, nationalism, fascism, and revanchism.

International affairs must be completely permeated with scientific methodology and a democratic spirit, with a fearless weighing of all facts, views, and theories, with maximum publicity of ultimate and intermediate goals, and with a consistency of principles.

# INTERNATIONAL TENSIONS AND NEW PRINCIPLES

The international policies of the world's two leading super-powers (the United States and the Soviet Union) must be based on a universal acceptance of unified and general principles, which we initially would formulate as follows:

All peoples have the right to decide their own fate with a free expression of will. This right is guaranteed by international control over observance by all governments of the "Declaration of the Rights of Man." International control presupposes the use of economic sanctions as well as the use of military forces of the United Nations in defense of "the rights of man."

All military and military-economic forms of export of revolution and counterrevolution are illegal and are tantamount to aggression.

All countries strive toward mutual help in economic,

cultural, and general-organizational problems with the aim of eliminating painlessly all domestic and international difficulties and preventing a sharpening of international tensions and a strengthening of the forces of reaction.

International policy does not aim at exploiting local, specific conditions to widen zones of influence and create difficulties for another country. The goal of international policy is to insure universal fulfillment of the "Declaration of the Rights of Man" and to prevent a sharpening of international tensions and a strengthening of militarist and nationalist tendencies.

□

Such a set of principles would in no way be a betrayal of the revolutionary and national liberation struggle, the struggle against reaction and counterrevolution. On the contrary, with the elimination of all doubtful cases, it would be easier to take decisive action in those extreme cases of reaction, racism, and militarism that allow no course other than armed struggle. A strengthening of peaceful coexistence would create an opportunity to avert such tragic events as those in Greece and Indonesia.

Such a set of principles would present the Soviet armed forces with a precisely defined defensive mission, a mission of defending our country and our allies from aggression. As history has shown, our people and their armed forces are unconquerable when they are defending their homeland and its great social and cultural achievements.

# HUNGER AND
OVERPOPULATION
(and the Psychology of Racism)

Specialists are paying attention to a growing threat of
hunger in the poorer half of the world. Although the 50
percent increase of the world's population in the last thirty
years has been accompanied by a 70 percent increase in
food production, the balance in the poorer half of the
world has been unfavorable. The situation in India, Indonesia, in a number of countries of Latin America, and in a
large number of other underdeveloped countries—the absence of technical-economic reserves, competent officials,
and cultural skills, social backwardness, a high birth rate—
systematically worsens the food balance and without doubt
will continue to worsen it in the coming years.

The answer would be a wide application of fertilizers,
an improvement of irrigation systems, better farm technology, wider use of the resources of the oceans, and a gradual

perfection of the production, already technically feasible, of synthetic foods, primarily amino acids. However, this is all fine for the rich nations. In the more backward countries, it is apparent from an analysis of the situation and existing trends that an improvement cannot be achieved in the near future, before the expected date of tragedy, 1975–80.

What is involved is a prognosticated deterioration of the average food balance in which localized food crises merge into a sea of hunger, intolerable suffering and desperation, the grief and fury of millions of people. This is a tragic threat to all mankind. A catastrophe of such dimension cannot but have profound consequences for the entire world and for every human being. It will provoke a wave of wars and hatred, a decline of standards of living throughout the world, and will leave a tragic, cynical, and anti-Communist mark on the life of future generations.

The first reaction of a philistine in hearing about the problem is that "they" are responsible for their plight because "they" reproduce so rapidly. Unquestionably, control of the birth rate is important and the people, in India for example, are taking steps in this direction. But these steps remain largely ineffective under social and economic backwardness, surviving traditions of large families, an absence of old-age benefits, a high infant mortality rate until quite recently, and a continuing threat of death from starvation.

It is apparently futile only to insist that the more backward countries restrict their birth rates. What is needed most of all is economic and technical assistance to these countries. This assistance must be of such scale and generosity that it is unlikely before the estrangement in the world and the egotistical, narrow-minded approach to relations between nations and races are eliminated. It is impossible as long as the United States and the Soviet Union, the world's two great super-powers, look upon each other as rivals and opponents.

Social factors play an important role in the tragic present situation and the still more tragic future of the impoverished regions. It must be clearly understood that if a threat of hunger is, along with a striving toward national independence, the main cause of "agrarian" revolution, the "agrarian" revolution in itself will not eliminate the threat of hunger, at least not in the immediate future. The threat of hunger cannot be eliminated without the assistance of the developed countries, and this requires significant changes in their foreign and domestic policies.

At this time, the white citizens of the United States are unwilling to accept even minimum sacrifices to eliminate the unequal economic and cultural position of the country's black citizens, who make up 10 percent of the population.

It is necessary to change the psychology of the American citizens so that they will voluntarily and generously support their government and worldwide efforts to change the economy, technology, and level of living of billions of people. This, of course, would entail a serious decline in the United States rate of economic growth. The Americans should be willing to do this solely for the sake of lofty and distant goals, for the sake of preserving civilization and mankind on our planet.

Similar changes in the psychology of people and practical activities of governments must be achieved in the Soviet Union and other developed countries.

In the opinion of the author, a fifteen-year tax equal to 20 percent of national incomes must be imposed on developed nations. The imposition of such a tax would automatically lead to a significant reduction in expenditures for weapons. Such common assistance would have an important effect—that of stabilizing and improving the situation in the most underdeveloped countries, restricting the influence of extremists of all types.

Changes in the economic situation of underdeveloped countries would solve the problem of high birth rates with relative ease, as has been shown by the experience of developed countries, without the barbaric method of sterilization.

Certain changes in the policies, viewpoints, and traditions on this delicate question are inescapable in the advanced countries as well. Mankind can develop smoothly only if it looks upon itself in a demographic sense as a unit, a single family without divisions into nations other than in matters of history and traditions.

Therefore, government policy, legislation on the family and marriage, and propaganda should not encourage an increase in the birth rates of advanced countries while demanding that it be curtailed in underdeveloped countries that are receiving assistance. Such a two-faced game would produce nothing but bitterness and nationalism.

In conclusion on that point, I want to emphasize that the question of regulating birth rates is highly complex and that any standardized, dogmatic solution "for all time and all peoples" would be wrong. All the foregoing, incidentally, should be accepted with the reservation that it is somewhat of a simplification.

# POLLUTION
# OF ENVIRONMENT

We live in a swiftly changing world. Industrial and water-engineering projects, cutting of forests, plowing up of virgin lands, the use of poisonous chemicals—all such activity is changing the face of the earth, our "habitat."

Scientific study of all the interrelationships in nature and the consequences of our interference clearly lags behind the changes. Large amounts of harmful wastes of industry and transport are being dumped into the air and water, including cancer-inducing substances. Will the safe limit be passed everywhere, as has already happened in a number of places?

Carbon dioxide from the burning of coal is altering the heat-reflecting qualities of the atmosphere. Sooner or later, this will reach a dangerous level. But we do not know when. Poisonous chemicals used in agriculture are penetrating the body of man and animal directly, and in more dangerous modified compounds are causing serious damage to the brain, the nervous system, blood-forming organs, the liver, and other organs. Here, too, the safe limit can be easily crossed, but the question has not been fully studied and it is difficult to control all these processes.

The use of antibiotics in poultry-raising has led to the development of new disease-causing microbes that are resistant to antibiotics.

I could also mention the problems of dumping detergents and radioactive wastes, erosion and salinization of soils, the flooding of meadows, the cutting of forests on mountain slopes and in watersheds, the destruction of birds and other useful wildlife like toads and frogs, and many other examples of senseless despoliation caused by local, temporary, bureaucratic, and egotistical interest and sometimes simply by questions of bureaucratic prestige, as in the sad fate of Lake Baikal.

The problem of geohygiene (earth hygiene) is highly complex and closely tied to economic and social problems. This problem can therefore not be solved on a national and especially not on a local basis. The salvation of our environment requires that we overcome our divisions and the pressure of temporary, local interests. Otherwise, the Soviet Union will poison the United States with its wastes and vice versa. At present, this is a hyperbole. But with a 10 percent annual increase of wastes, the increase over a hundred years will be multiplied twenty thousand times.

# POLICE DICTATORSHIPS

An extreme reflection of the dangers confronting modern social development is the growth of racism, nationalism, and militarism and, in particular, the rise of demagogic, hypocritical, and monstrously cruel dictatorial police regimes. Foremost are the regimes of Stalin, Hitler, and Mao Tse-tung, and a number of extremely reactionary regimes in smaller countries, such as Spain, Portugal, South Africa, Greece, Albania, Haiti, and other Latin American countries.

These tragic developments have always derived from the struggle of egotistical and group interests, the struggle for unlimited power, suppression of intellectual freedom, a spread of intellectually simplified, narrow-minded mass myths (the myth of race, of land and blood, the myth about the Jewish danger, anti-intellectualism, the concept of *lebensraum* in Germany, the myth about the sharpening of the class struggle and proletarian infallibility bolstered by the cult of Stalin and by exaggeration of the contradictions with capitalism in the Soviet Union, the myth about Mao Tse-tung, extreme Chinese nationalism and the resurrection of the *lebensraum* concept, of anti-intellectualism, extreme anti-humanism, and certain prejudices of peasant socialism in China).

The usual practice is the use of demagogy, storm troopers, and Red Guards in the first stage and terrorist bureaucracy with reliable cadres of the type of Eichmann, Himmler, Yezhov, and Beria at the summit of deification of unlimited power.

The world will never forget the burning of books in the squares of German cities, the hysterical, cannibalistic speeches of the fascist "führers," and their even more cannibalistic plans for the destruction of entire peoples, including the Russians. Fascism began a partial realization of these plans during the war it unleashed, annihilating prisoners of war and hostages, burning villages, carrying out a criminal policy of genocide (during the war, the main blow of genocide was aimed at the Jews, a policy that apparently was also meant to be provocative, especially in the Ukraine and Poland).

We shall never forget the kilometer-long trenches filled with bodies, the gas chambers, the SS dogs, the fanatical doctors, the piles of women's hair, suitcases with gold teeth, and fertilizer from the factories of death.

Analyzing the causes of Hitler's coming to power, we will never forget the role of German and international monopolist capital. We also will not forget the criminally sectarian and dogmatically narrow policies of Stalin and his associates, setting Socialists and Communists against one another (this has been well related in the famous letter to Ilya Ehrenburg by Ernst Henri).*

Fascism lasted twelve years in Germany. Stalinism lasted twice as long in the Soviet Union. There are many common features but also certain differences. Stalinism exhibited a much more subtle kind of hypocrisy and demagogy, with reliance not on an openly cannibalistic program like Hitler's but on a progressive, scientific, and popular socialist ideology.

This served as a convenient screen for deceiving the working class, for weakening the vigilance of the intellectuals and other rivals in the struggle for power, with the treacherous and sudden use of the machinery of torture, execution, and informants, intimidating and making fools of millions of people, the majority of whom were neither cowards nor fools. As a consequence of this "specific feature" of Stalinism, it was the Soviet people, its most active, talented, and honest representatives, who suffered the most terrible blow.

At least ten to fifteen million people perished in the torture chambers of the NKVD [secret police] from torture and execution, in camps for exiled kulaks [rich peasants] and so-called semi-kulaks and members of their families and in camps "without the right of correspondence" (which were in fact the prototypes of the fascist death camps, where, for example, thousands of prisoners were machine-

---

* Ernst Henri, a German Communist long resident in the Soviet Union, outlined in this letter the role Stalin's policies had played in making possible Hitler's rise—notably his insistence that the German Communist Party view as its chief enemy the German Social Democratic Party rather than Hitler's Nazis. Henri's thesis was that the German Communists and Social Democrats should have formed a united front against Hitler.

gunned because of "overcrowding" or as a result of "special orders").

People perished in the mines of Norilsk and Vorkuta from freezing, starvation, and exhausting labor, at countless construction projects, in timber-cutting, building of canals, or simply during transportation in prison trains, in the overcrowded holds of "death ships" in the Sea of Okhotsk, and during the resettlement of entire peoples, the Crimean Tatars, the Volga Germans, the Kalmyks, and other Caucasus peoples. Readers of the literary journal *Novy Mir* recently could read for themselves a description of the "road of death" between Norilsk and Igarka [in northern Siberia].

Temporary masters were replaced (Yagoda, Molotov, Yezhov, Zhdanov, Malenkov, Beria), but the anti-people's regime of Stalin remained equally cruel and at the same time dogmatically narrow and blind in its cruelty. The killing of military and engineering officials before the war, the blind faith in the "reasonableness" of the colleague in crime, Hitler, and the other reasons for the national tragedy of 1941 have been well described in the book by Nekrich, in the notes of Maj. Gen. Grigorenko, and other publications—these are far from the only examples of the combination of crime, narrow-mindedness, and short-sightedness.*

Stalinist dogmatism and isolation from real life was demonstrated particularly in the countryside, in the policy

---

* A. M. Nekrich, a distinguished Soviet historian, was expelled from the Soviet Communist Party after publishing a study of Stalin's errors and unpreparedness for the Nazi attack of June 1941. Maj. Gen. Pyotr G. Grigorenko, author of a long memorandum supporting Nekrich and a leading Soviet dissident, has been confined as punishment in Soviet mental hospitals.

of unlimited exploitation and the predatory forced deliveries at "symbolic" prices, in almost serflike enslavement of the peasantry, the depriving of peasants of the simplest means of mechanization, and the appointment of collective-farm chairmen on the basis of their cunning and obsequiousness. The results are evident—a profound and hard-to-correct destruction of the economy and way of life in the countryside, which, by the law of interconnected vessels, damaged industry as well.

The inhuman character of Stalinism was demonstrated by the repressions of prisoners of war who survived fascist camps and then were thrown into Stalinist camps, the anti-worker "decrees," the criminal exile of entire peoples condemned to slow death, the unenlightened zoological kind of anti-Semitism that was characteristic of Stalin bureaucracy and the NKVD (and Stalin personally), the Ukrainophobia characteristic of Stalin, and the draconian laws for the protection of socialist property (five years' imprisonment for stealing some grain from the fields and so forth) that served mainly as a means of fulfilling the demands of the "slave market."

A profound analysis of the origin and development of Stalinism is contained in the thousand-page monograph of Roy Medvedev.[*] This was written from a socialist, Marxist point of view and is a successful work, but unfortunately it has not yet been published. The present author is not likely to receive such a compliment from Comrade Medvedev, who finds elements of "Westernism" in his views. Well, there is nothing like controversy! Actually the views of the

[*] Medvedev's study was published in the United States and Britain in 1972 under the title *Let History Judge*.

present author are profoundly socialist, and he hopes that the attentive reader will understand this.

The author is quite aware of the monstrous relations in human and international affairs brought forth by the egotistical principle of capital when it is not under pressure from socialist and progressive forces. He also thinks, however, that progressives in the West understand this better than he does and are waging a struggle against these manifestations. The author is concentrating his attention on what is before his eyes and on what is obstructing, from his point of view, a worldwide overcoming of estrangement, obstructing the struggle for democracy, social progress, and intellectual freedom.

Our country has started on the path of cleansing away the foulness of Stalinism. "We are squeezing the slave out of ourselves drop by drop" (an expression of Anton Chekhov). We are learning to express our opinions, without taking the lead from the bosses and without fearing for our lives.

The beginning of this arduous and far from straight path evidently dates from the report of Nikita S. Khrushchev to the Twentieth Congress of the Soviet Communist Party. This bold speech, which came as a surprise to Stalin's accomplices in crime, and a number of associated measures —the release of hundreds of thousands of political prisoners and their rehabilitation, steps toward a revival of the principles of peaceful coexistence and toward a revival of democracy—oblige us to value highly the historic role of Khrushchev despite his regrettable mistakes of a voluntarist character in subsequent years and despite the fact that Khrushchev, while Stalin was alive, was one of his collaborators in crime, occupying a number of influential posts.

The exposure of Stalinism in our country still has a long way to go. It is imperative, of course, that we publish all authentic documents, including the archives of the NKVD, and conduct nationwide investigations. It would be highly useful for the international authority of the Soviet Communist Party and the ideals of socialism if, as was planned in 1964 but never carried out, the party were to announce the "symbolic" expulsion of Stalin, murderer of millions of Party members, and at the same time the political rehabilitation of the victims of Stalinism.

From 1936 to 1939 more than 1.2 million Party members, half of the total membership, were arrested. Only fifty thousand regained freedom; the others were tortured during interrogation or were shot (six hundred thousand) or died in camps. Only in isolated cases were the rehabilitated allowed to assume responsible posts; even fewer were permitted to take part in the investigation of crimes of which they had been witnesses or victims.

We are often told lately not to "rub salt into wounds." This is usually being said by people who suffered no wounds. Actually only the most meticulous analysis of the past and of its consequences will now enable us to wash off the blood and dirt that befouled our banner.

It is sometimes suggested in the literature that the political manifestations of Stalinism represented a sort of superstructure over the economic basis of an anti-Leninist pseudosocialism that led to the formation in the Soviet Union of a distinct class—a bureaucratic elite from which all key positions are filled and which is rewarded for its work through open and concealed privileges. I cannot deny that there is some (but not the whole) truth in such an interpretation, which would help explain the vitality of neo-Stalinism, but a full analysis of this issue would go beyond the scope of this essay, which focuses on another aspect of the problem.

It is imperative that we restrict in every possible way the influence of neo-Stalinists in our political life. Here we are compelled to mention a specific person. One of the most influential representatives of neo-Stalinism at the present time is the director of the Science Department of the Communist Party's Central Committee, Sergei P. Trapeznikov. The leadership of our country and our people should know that the views of this unquestionably intelligent, shrewd, and highly consistent man are basically Stalinist (from our point of view, they reflect the interests of the bureaucratic elite).

His views differ fundamentally from the dreams and aspirations of the majority and most active section of the intelligentsia, which, in our opinion, reflect the true interests of all our people and progressive mankind. The leadership of our country should understand that as long as such a man (if I correctly understand the nature of his views) exercises influence, it is impossible to hope for a strengthening of the Party's position among scientific and artistic intellectuals. An indication of this was given at the last elections in the Academy of Sciences when Trapeznikov was rejected by a substantial majority of votes, but this hint was not "understood" by the leadership.

The issue does not involve the professional or personal qualities of Trapeznikov, about which I know little. The issue involves his political views. I have based the foregoing on word-of-mouth evidence. Therefore, I cannot in principle exclude the possibility (although it is unlikely) that in reality everything is quite the opposite. In that pleasant event, I would beg forgiveness and retract what I have written.

In recent years, demagogy, violence, cruelty, and vileness have seized a great country embarked on the path of socialist development. I refer, of course, to China. It is impossible without horror and pain to read about the mass contagion of anti-humanism being spread by "the great helmsman" and his accomplices, about the Red Guards who, according to the Chinese radio, "jumped with joy" during public executions of "ideological enemies" of Chairman Mao.

The idiocy of the cult of personality has assumed in China monstrous, grotesquely tragicomic forms, carrying to the point of absurdity many of the traits of Stalinism and Hitlerism. But this absurdity has proved effective in making fools of tens of millions of people and in destroying and humiliating millions of intelligent citizens.

The full picture of the tragedy in China is unclear. But in any case, it is impossible to look at it in isolation from the internal economic difficulties of China after the collapse of the adventure of "the great leap forward," in isolation from the struggle by various groups for power, or in isolation from the foreign political situation—the war in Vietnam, the estrangement in the world, and the inadequate and lagging struggle against Stalinism in the Soviet Union.

The greatest damage from Maoism is often seen in the split of the world Communist movement. That is, of course, not so. The split is the result of a disease and to some extent represents the way to treat that disease. In the presence of the disease a formal unity would have been a dangerous, unprincipled compromise that would have led the world Communist movement into a blind alley once and for all.

Actually the crimes of the Maoists against human

rights have gone much too far, and the Chinese people are now in much greater need of help from the world's democratic forces to defend their rights than in need of the unity of the world's Communist forces, in the Maoist sense, for the purpose of combating the so-called imperialist peril somewhere in Africa or in Latin America or in the Middle East.

# THE THREAT TO
# INTELLECTUAL FREEDOM

This is a threat to the independence and worth of the human personality, a threat to the meaning of human life.

Nothing threatens freedom of the personality and the meaning of life like war, poverty, terror. But there are also indirect and only slightly more remote dangers.

One of these is the stupefaction of man (the "gray mass," to use the cynical term of bourgeois prognosticators) by mass culture with its intentional or commercially motivated lowering of intellectual level and content, with its stress on entertainment or utilitarianism, and with its carefully protective censorship.

Another example is related to the question of education. A system of education under government control, separation of school and church, universal free education— all these are great achievements of social progress. But everything has a reverse side. In this case it is excessive standardization, extending to the teaching process itself, to the curriculum, especially in literature, history, civics, geography, and to the system of examinations.

One cannot but see a danger in excessive reference to authority and in the limitation of discussion and intellectual boldness at an age when personal convictions are beginning to be formed. In the old China, the systems of examinations for official positions led to mental stagnation and to the canonizing of the reactionary aspects of Confucianism. It is highly undesirable to have anything like that in a modern society.

Modern technology and mass psychology constantly suggest new possibilities of managing the norms of behavior, the strivings and convictions of masses of people. This involves not only management through information based on the theory of advertising and mass psychology, but also more technical methods that are widely discussed in the press abroad. Examples are biochemical control of the birth rate and biochemical and electronic control of psychic processes.

It seems to me that we cannot completely ignore these new methods or prohibit the progress of science and technology, but we must be clearly aware of the awesome danger to basic human values and to the meaning of life that may be concealed in the misuse of technical and biochemical methods and the methods of mass psychology.

Man must not be turned into a chicken or a rat as in the well-known experiments in which elation is induced electrically through electrodes inserted into the brain. Related to this is the question of the ever-increasing use of tranquilizers and anti-depressants, legal and illegal narcotics, and so forth.

We also must not forget the very real danger mentioned by Norbert Wiener in his book *Cybernetics*, namely the absence in cybernetic machines of stable human norms of behavior. The tempting, unprecedented power that mankind, or, even worse, a particular group in a divided mankind, may derive from the wise counsels of its future intellectual aides, the artificial "thinking" automata, may become, as Wiener warned, a fatal trap; the counsels may turn out to be incredibly insidious and, instead of pursuing human objectives, may pursue completely abstract problems that had been transformed in an unforeseen manner in the artificial brain.

Such a danger will become quite real in a few decades if human values, particularly freedom of thought, are not strengthened, if alienation is not eliminated.

Let us now return for the dangers of today, to the need for intellectual freedom, which will enable the public at large and the intelligentsia to control and assess all acts, designs, and decisions of the ruling group.

Marx once wrote that the illusion that the "bosses know everything best" and "only the higher circles familiar with the official nature of things can pass judgment" was held by officials who equate the public weal with governmental authority.

Both Marx and Lenin always stressed the viciousness of a bureaucratic system as the opposite of a democratic system. Lenin used to say that every cook should learn how to govern. Now the diversity and complexity of social phenomena and the dangers facing mankind have become immeasurably greater; and it is therefore all the more important that mankind be protected against the danger of dogmatic and voluntaristic errors, which are inevitable when decisions are reached in a closed circle of secret advisers or shadow cabinets.

It is no wonder that the problem of censorship (in the broadest sense of the word) has been one of the central issues in the ideological struggle of the last few years. Here is what a progressive American sociologist, Lewis A. Coser, has to say on this point:

"It would be absurd to attribute the alienation of many avant-garde authors solely to the battle with the censors; yet one may well maintain that those battles contributed in no mean measure to such alienation. To these authors, the censor came to be the very symbol of the Philistinism, hypocrisy and meanness of bourgeois society.

"Many an author who was initially apolitical was drawn to the political left in the United States because the left was in the forefront of the battle against censorship. The close alliance of avant-garde art with avant-garde political and social radicalism can be accounted for, at least in part, by the fact that they came to be merged in the mind of many as a single battle for freedom against all repression." (I quote from an article by Igor Kon, published in *Novy Mir* in January 1968.)

We are all familiar with the passionate and closely argued appeal against censorship by the outstanding Soviet writer A. Solzhenitsyn. He as well as G. Vladimov, G. Svirsky, and other writers who have spoken out on the subject has clearly shown how incompetent censorship destroys the living soul of Soviet literature; but the same applies, of course, to all other manifestations of social thought, causing stagnation and dullness and preventing fresh and deep ideas.

Such ideas, after all, can arise only in discussion, in the face of objections, only if there is a potential possibility of expressing not only true but also dubious ideas. This was clear to the philosophers of ancient Greece and hardly anyone nowadays would have any doubts on that score. But after fifty years of complete domination over the minds of an entire nation, our leaders seem to fear even allusions to such a discussion.

At this point we must touch on some disgraceful tendencies that have become evident in the last few years. We will cite only a few isolated examples without trying to create a whole picture. The crippling censorship of Soviet artistic and political literature has again been intensified. Dozens of brilliant writings cannot see the light of day. They include some of the best of Solzhenitsyn's works, executed with great artistic and moral force and containing profound artistic and philosophical generalizations. Is this not a disgrace?

Wide indignation has been aroused by the recent decree adopted by the Supreme Soviet of the Russian Republic amending the Criminal Code in direct contravention of the civil rights proclaimed by our Constitution. [The decree included literary protests among acts punishable under Article 190, which deals with failure to report crimes.]

The Daniel-Sinyavsky trial, which has been condemned by the progressive public in the Soviet Union and abroad (from Louis Aragon to Graham Greene) and has compromised the Communist system, has still not been reviewed. The two writers languish in a camp with a strict regime and are being subjected (especially Daniel) to harsh humiliations and ordeals.*

* Yuli M. Daniel and Andrei D. Sinyavsky were convicted in 1966 of smuggling out of the Soviet Union literary works that the authorities contended were slanderous to the Soviet state. The trial aroused widespread concern both within and outside the Soviet Union. After more than five years in Soviet prison camps the men were released. Sinyavsky is now living in France.

Most political prisoners are now kept in a group of camps in the Mordvinian Republic, where the total number of prisoners, including criminals, is about fifty thousand. According to available information, the regime has become increasingly severe in these camps, with personnel left over from Stalinist times playing an increasing role. It should be said, in all fairness, that a certain improvement has been noted very recently; it is to be hoped that this turn of events will continue.

The restoration of Leninist principles of public control over places of imprisonment would undoubtedly be a healthy development. Equally important would be a complete amnesty for political prisoners, and not just the recent limited amnesty, which was proclaimed on the fiftieth anniversary of the October Revolution as a result of a temporary victory of rightist tendencies in our leadership. There should also be a review of all political trials that are still raising doubts among the progressive public.

Was it not disgraceful to allow the arrest, twelve-month detention without trial, and then the conviction and sentencing to terms of five to seven years of Ginzburg, Galanskov, and others for activities that actually amounted to a defense of civil liberties and (partly, as an example) of Daniel and Sinyavsky personally. The author of these lines sent an appeal to the Party's Central Committee on February 11, 1967, asking that the Ginzburg-Galanskov case be closed. He received no reply and no explanations on the substance of the case. It was only later that he heard there had been an attempt (apparently inspired by Semichastny, the former chairman of the KGB) to slander the present writer and several other persons on the basis of inspired false testimony by one of the accused in the Ginzburg-Galanskov case. Subsequently the testimony of that person

—Dobrovolsky—was used at the trial as evidence to show that Ginzburg and Galanskov had ties with a foreign anti-Soviet organization, which one cannot help but doubt.

Was it not disgraceful to permit the conviction and sentencing (to three years in camps) of Khaustov and Bukovsky for participation in a meeting in defense of their comrades? Was it not disgraceful to allow persecution, in the best witch-hunt tradition, of dozens of members of the Soviet intelligentsia who spoke out against the arbitrariness of judicial and psychiatric agencies, to attempt to force honorable people to sign false, hypocritical "retractions," to dismiss and blacklist people, to deprive young writers, editors, and other members of the intelligentsia of all means of existence?*

Here is a typical example of this kind of activity.

Comrade B., a woman editor of books on motion pictures, was summoned to the Party's district committee. The first question was, "Who gave you the letter in defense of Ginzburg to sign?" "Allow me not to reply to that question," she answered.

"All right, you can go, we want to talk this over," she was told.

The decision was to expel the woman from the Party and to recommend that she be dismissed from her job and barred from working anywhere else in the field of culture.

With such methods of persuasion and indoctrination the Party can hardly expect to claim the role of spiritual leader of mankind.

---

* Aleksandr Ginzburg, a young poet, and Yury Galanskov, a poet and editor, were convicted on charges growing out of their protest of the Daniel-Sinyavsky case. Galanskov subsequently died in a prison camp. Vladimir Bukovsky and Yevgeny Kushev were arrested for protesting the Ginzburg-Galanskov case.

Was it not disgraceful to have the speech at the Moscow Party conference by the president of the Academy of Sciences [Mstislav V. Keldysh], who is evidently either too intimidated or too dogmatic in his views? Is it not disgraceful to allow another backsliding into anti-Semitism in our appointments policy (incidentally, in the highest bureaucratic elite of our government, the spirit of anti-Semitism was never fully dispelled after the 1930's).

Was it not disgraceful to continue to restrict the civil rights of the Crimean Tatars, who lost about 46 percent of their numbers (mainly children and old people) in the Stalinist repressions? Nationality problems will continue to be a reason for unrest and dissatisfaction unless all departures from Leninist principles are acknowledged and analyzed and firm steps are taken to correct mistakes.

Is it not highly disgraceful and dangerous to make increasingly frequent attempts, either directly or indirectly (through silence), to publicly rehabilitate Stalin, his associates, and his policy, his pseudosocialism of terroristic bureaucracy, a socialism of hypocrisy and ostentatious growth that was at best a quantitative and one-sided growth involving the loss of many qualitative features? (This is a reference to the basic tendencies and consequences of Stalin's policy, or Stalinism, rather than a comprehensive assessment of the entire diversified situation in a huge country with two hundred million people.)

Although all these disgraceful phenomena are still far from the monstrous scale of the crimes of Stalinism and rather resemble in scope the sadly famous McCarthyism of the cold war era, the Soviet public cannot but be highly disturbed and indignant and display vigilance even in the face of insignificant manifestations of neo-Stalinism in our country.

We are convinced that the world's Communists will also view negatively any attempt to revive Stalinism in our country, which would, after all, be an awful blow to the attractive force of Communist ideas throughout the world.

Today the key to a progressive restructuring of the system of government in the interests of mankind lies in intellectual freedom. This has been understood, in particular, by the Czechoslovaks and there can be no doubt that we should support their bold initiative, which is so valuable for the future of socialism and all mankind. That support should be political and, in the early stages, include increased economic aid.

The situation involving censorship (Glavlit) in our country is such that it can hardly be corrected for any length of time simply by "liberalized" directives. Major organizational and legislative measures are required, for example, adoption of a special law on press and information that would clearly and convincingly define what can and what cannot be printed and would place the responsibility on competent people who would be under public control. It is essential that the exchange of information on an international scale (press, tourism, and so forth) be expanded in every way, that we get to know ourselves better, that we not try to save on sociological, political, and economic research and surveys, that we not restrict our research to that done in a government-controlled program (otherwise we might be tempted to avoid "unpleasant" subjects and questions).

# THE BASIS FOR HOPE

## PEACEFUL COMPETITION

The prospects of socialism now depend on whether socialism can be made attractive, whether the moral attractiveness of the ideas of socialism and the glorification of labor, compared with the egotistical ideas of private ownership and the glorification of capital, will be the decisive factors that people will bear in mind when comparing socialism and capitalism, or whether people will remember mainly the limitations of intellectual freedom under socialism or, even worse, the fascistic regime of the cult [of personality].

I am placing the accent on the moral aspect because, when it comes to achieving a high productivity of social labor or developing all productive forces or insuring a high standard of living for most of the population, capitalism and socialism seem to have "played to a tie." Let us examine this question in detail.

Imagine two skiers racing through deep snow. At the start of the race, one of them, in a striped jacket, was many kilometers ahead, but now the skier in the red jacket is catching up to the leader. What can we say about their relative strength? Not very much, since each skier is racing under different conditions. The striped one broke the snow, and the red one did not have to. (The reader will understand that this ski race symbolizes the burden of research and development costs that the country leading in technology has to bear.) All one can say about the race is that there is not much difference in strength between the two skiers.

The parable does not, of course, reflect the whole complexity of comparing economic and technological progress in the United States and the Soviet Union, the relative vitality of RRS and AME (Russian Revolutionary Sweep and American Efficiency).

We cannot forget that during much of the period in question the Soviet Union waged a hard war and then healed its wounds; we cannot forget that some absurdities in our development were not an inherent aspect of the socialist course of development but a tragic accident, a serious, though not inevitable, disease.

On the other hand, any comparison must take account of the fact that we are now catching up with the United States only in some of the old, traditional industries, which are no longer as important as they used to be for the United States (for example, coal and steel). In some of the newer fields—for example, automation, computers, petrochemicals, and especially in industrial research and development —we are not only lagging behind but are also growing more slowly, so that a complete victory of our economy in the next few decades is unlikely.

It must also be borne in mind that our nation is endowed with vast natural resources, from fertile black earth to coal and forests, from oil to manganese and diamonds. It must be borne in mind that during the period under review our people worked to the limit of their capacity, which resulted in a certain depletion of resources.

We must also bear in mind the ski-track effect, in which the Soviet Union adopted principles of industrial organization and technology and development previously tested in the United States. Examples are the method of calculating the national fuel budget, assembly-line techniques, antibiotics, nuclear power, oxygen converters in steel-making, hybrid corn, self-propelled harvester combines, strip mining of coal, rotary excavators, semiconductors in electronics, the shift from steam to diesel locomotives, and much more.

There is only one justifiable conclusion and it can be formulated cautiously as follows:

1. We have demonstrated the vitality of the socialist course, which has done a great deal for the people materially, culturally, and socially and, like no other system, has glorified the moral significance of labor.

2. There are no grounds for asserting, as is often done in the dogmatic vein, that the capitalist mode of production leads the economy into a blind alley or that it is obviously inferior to the socialist mode in labor productivity, and there are certainly no grounds for asserting that capitalism always leads to absolute impoverishment of the working class.

The continuing economic progress being achieved under capitalism should be a fact of great theoretical significance for any nondogmatic Marxist. It is precisely this

fact that lies at the basis of peaceful coexistence and it sug-
gests, in principle, that if capitalism ever runs into an economic blind alley it will not necessarily have to leap into a
desperate military adventure. Both capitalism and socialism
are capable of long-term development, borrowing positive
elements from each other, and actually coming closer to
each other in a number of essential aspects.

I can just hear the outcries about revisionism and
blunting of the class approach to this issue; I can just see the
smirks about political naïveté and immaturity. But the facts
suggest that there is real economic progress in the United
States and other capitalist countries, that the capitalists are
actually using the social principles of socialism, and that
there has been real improvement in the position of the
working people. More important, the facts suggest that on
any other course except ever-increasing coexistence and
collaboration between the two systems and the two super-
powers, with a smoothing of contradictions and with mutual assistance, on any other course annihilation awaits
mankind. There is no other way out.

We will now compare the distribution of personal income and consumption for various social groups in the
United States and the Soviet Union. Our propaganda materials usually assert that there is crying inequality in the
United States, while the Soviet Union has something entirely just, entirely in the interests of the working people.
Actually both statements contain half truths and a fair
amount of hypocritical evasion.

I have no intention of minimizing the tragic aspects of
the poverty, lack of rights, and humiliation of the twenty-
two million American Negroes. But we must clearly understand that this problem is not primarily a class problem, but

a racial problem, involving the racism and egotism of white workers, and that the ruling group in the United States is interested in solving this problem. To be sure, the government has not been as active as it should be; this may be related to fears of an electoral character and to fears of upsetting the unstable equilibrium in the country and thus activating extreme leftist and especially extreme rightist parties. It seems to me that we in the socialist camp should be interested in letting the ruling group in the United States settle the Negro problem without aggravating the situation in the country.

At the other extreme, the presence of millionaires in the United States is not a serious economic burden in view of their small number. The total consumption of the rich is less than 20 percent, that is, less than the total rise of national consumption over a five-year period. From this point of view, a revolution, which would be likely to halt economic progress for more than five years, does not appear to be an economically advantageous move for the working people. And I am not even talking of the bloodletting that is inevitable in a revolution. And I am not talking of the danger of the "irony of history," about which Friedrich Engels wrote so well in his famous letter to V. Zasulich, the "irony" that took the form of Stalinism in our country.

There are, of course, situations where revolution is the only way out. This applies especially to national uprisings. But that is not the case in the United States and other developed capitalist countries, as suggested, incidentally, in the programs of the Communist parties of these countries.

As far as our country is concerned, here, too, we should avoid painting an idyllic picture. There is still great inequality in property between the city and the countryside, especially in rural areas that lack a transport outlet to the private market or do not produce any goods in demand in private trade. There are great differences between cities with some of the new, privileged industries and those with older, antiquated industries. As a result, 40 percent of the Soviet population is in difficult economic circumstances. In the United States about 25 percent of the population is on the verge of poverty. On the other hand, the 5 percent of the Soviet population that belongs to the managerial group is as privileged as its counterpart in the United States.

The development of modern society in both the Soviet Union and the United States is now following the same course of increasing complexity of structure and of industrial management, giving rise in both countries to managerial groups that are similar in social character.

We must therefore acknowledge that there is no qualitative difference in the structure of society of the two countries in terms of distribution of consumption. Unfortunately, the effectiveness of the managerial group in the Soviet Union (and, to a lesser extent, in the United States) is measured not only in purely economic or productive terms. This group also performs a concealed protective function that is rewarded in the sphere of consumption by concealed privileges.

Few people are aware of the practice under Stalin of paying salaries in sealed envelopes, of the constantly recurring concealed distribution of scarce foods and goods for various services, privileges in vacation resorts, and so forth.

I want to emphasize that I am not opposed to the socialist principle of payment based on the amount and quality of labor. Relatively higher wages for better administrators, for highly skilled workers, teachers, and physicians, for workers in dangerous or harmful occupations, for workers in science, culture, and the arts, all of whom account for a relatively small part of the total wage bill, do not threaten society if they are not accompanied by concealed privileges; moreover, higher wages benefit society if they are deserved.

The point is that every wasted minute of a leading administrator represents a major material loss for the economy, and every wasted minute of a leading figure in the arts means a loss in the emotional, philosophical, and artistic wealth of society. But when something is done in secret, the suspicion inevitably arises that things are not clean, that loyal servants of the existing system are being bribed.

It seems to me that the rational way of solving this touchy problem would be not the setting of income ceilings for Party members or some such measure, but simply the prohibition of all privileges and the establishment of unified wage rates based on the social value of labor and an economic market approach to the wage problem.

I consider that further advances in our economic reform and a greater role for economic and market factors accompanied by increased public control over the managerial group (which, incidentally, is also essential in capitalist countries) will help eliminate all the roughness in our present distribution pattern.

An even more important aspect of the economic reform for the regulation and stimulation of production is the establishment of a correct system of market prices, proper allocation and rapid utilization of investment funds, and proper use of natural and human resources based on appropriate rents in the interest of our society.

A number of socialist countries, including the Soviet

Union, Yugoslavia, and Czechoslovakia, are now experimenting with basic economic problems of the role of planning and of the market, government and cooperative ownership, and so forth. These experiments are of great significance.

Summing up, we now come to our basic conclusion about the moral and ethical character of the advantages of the socialist course of development of human society. In our view, this does not in any way minimize the significance of socialism. Without socialism, bourgeois practices and the egotistical principle of private ownership gave rise to the "people of the abyss" described by Jack London and earlier by Engels.

Only the competition with socialism and the pressure of the working class made possible the social progress of the twentieth century and, all the more, will insure the now inevitable process of rapprochement of the two systems. It took socialism to raise the meaning of labor to the heights of a moral feat. Before the advent of socialism, national egotism gave rise to colonial oppression, nationalism, and racism. By now it has become clear that victory is on the side of the humanistic, international approach.

The capitalist world could not help giving birth to the socialist, but now the socialist world should not seek to destroy by force the ground from which it grew. Under the present conditions this would be tantamount to the suicide of mankind. Socialism should ennoble that ground by its example and other indirect forms of pressure and then merge with it.

The rapprochement with the capitalist world should not be an unprincipled, anti-popular plot between ruling groups, as happened in the extreme case [of the Soviet-Nazi rapprochement] of 1939–40. Such a rapprochement must rest not only on a socialist, but also on a popular, democratic foundation, under the control of public opinion, as expressed through publicity, elections, and so forth.

Such a rapprochement implies not only wide social reforms in the capitalist countries, but also substantial changes in the structure of ownership, with a greater role played by government and cooperative ownership, and the preservation of the basic features of ownership of the means of production in the socialist countries.

Our allies along this road are not only the working class and the progressive intelligentsia, which are interested in peaceful coexistence and social progress and in a democratic, peaceful transition to socialism (as reflected in the programs of the Communist parties of the developed countries), but also the reformist part of the bourgeoisie, which supports such a program of "convergence." (Although I am using this term, taken from Western literature, it is clear from the foregoing that I have given it a socialist and democratic meaning.)

Typical representatives of the reformist bourgeoisie are Cyrus Eaton, President Franklin D. Roosevelt and, especially, President John F. Kennedy. Without wishing to cast a stone in the direction of Comrade N. S. Khrushchev (our high esteem of his services was expressed earlier), I cannot help recalling one of his statements, which may have been more typical of his entourage than of him personally.

On July 10, 1961, in speaking at a reception of specialists about his meeting with Kennedy in Vienna, Comrade Khrushchev recalled Kennedy's request that the Soviet Union, in conducting policy and making demands, consider the actual possibilities and the difficulties of the new Kennedy administration and refrain from demanding more than it could grant without courting the danger of being defeated in elections and being replaced by rightist forces. At that time, Khrushchev did not give Kennedy's unprecedented request the proper attention, to put it mildly, and began to rail. And now, after the shots in Dallas, who can say what auspicious opportunities in world history have been, if not destroyed, at any rate set back because of a lack of understanding?

Bertrand Russell once told a peace congress in Moscow that "the world will be saved from thermonuclear annihilation if the leaders of each of the two systems prefer complete victory of the other system to a thermonuclear war." (I am quoting from memory.) It seems to me that such a solution would be acceptable to the majority of people in any country, whether capitalist or socialist. I consider that the leaders of the capitalist and socialist systems by the very nature of things will gradually be forced to adopt the point of view of the majority of mankind.

Intellectual freedom of society will facilitate and smooth the way for this trend toward patience, flexibility, and a security from dogmatism, fear, and adventurism. All mankind, including its best-organized and most active forces, the working class and the intelligentsia, is interested in freedom and security.

# A FOUR-STAGE PLAN FOR COOPERATION

Having examined the development of mankind according to the negative alternative, leading to annihilation, we must now attempt, even schematically, to suggest the positive alternative. (The author concedes the primitiveness of his attempts at prognostication, which requires the joint efforts of many specialists and here, even more than elsewhere, invites criticism.)

□

In the first stage, a growing ideological struggle in the socialist countries between Stalinist and Maoist forces, on the one hand, and the realistic forces of leftist Leninist Communists (and leftist Westerners), on the other, will lead to a deep ideological split on an international, national, and intraparty scale.

In the Soviet Union and other socialist countries, this process will lead first to a multiparty system (here and there) and to acute ideological struggle and discussions, and then to the ideological victory of the realists, affirming the policy of increasing peaceful coexistence, strengthening democracy, and expanding economic reforms (1968–80). The dates reflect the most optimistic unrolling of events.

The author, incidentally, is not one of those who consider the multiparty system to be an essential stage in the development of the socialist system, or, even less, a panacea for all ills, but he assumes that in some cases a multiparty system may be an inevitable consequence of the course of events when a ruling Communist Party refuses for one reason or another to rule by the scientific democratic method required by history.

□

In the second stage, persistent demands for social progress and peaceful coexistence in the United States and other capitalist countries, and pressure exerted by the example of the socialist countries and by internal progressive forces (the working class and the intelligentsia), will lead to the victory of the leftist reformist wing of the bourgeoisie, which will begin to implement a program of rapprochement (convergence) with socialism, i.e., social progress, peaceful coexistence, and collaboration with socialism on a world scale and changes in the structure of ownership. This phase includes an expanded role for the intelligentsia and an attack on the forces of racism and militarism (1972–85). (The various stages overlap.)

□

In the third stage, the Soviet Union and the United States, having overcome their alienation, solve the problem of saving the poorer half of the world. The aforementioned 20 percent tax on the national income of developed countries is applied. Gigantic fertilizer factories and irrigation systems using atomic power will be built [in the developing countries], the resources of the sea will be used to a vastly greater extent, indigenous personnel will be trained, and industrialization will be carried out. Gigantic factories will produce synthetic amino acids and synthesize proteins, fats, and carbohydrates. At the same time disarmament will proceed (1972–90).

□

In the fourth stage, the socialist convergence will reduce differences in social structure, promote intellectual freedom, science, and economic progress, and lead to the creation of a world government and the smoothing of national contradictions (1980–2000). During this period decisive progress can be expected in the field of nuclear power, on the basis of both uranium and thorium and, probably, deuterium and lithium.

Some authors consider it likely that explosive breeding (the reproduction of active materials such as plutonium, uranium 233, and tritium) may be used in subterranean or other enclosed explosions.

During this period the expansion of space exploration will require thousands of people to work and live continuously on other planets and on the moon, on artificial satellites and on asteroids whose orbits will have been changed by nuclear explosions.

The synthesis of materials that are super-conductors at room temperature may completely revolutionize electrical technology, cybernetics, transportation, and communications. Progress in biology (in this and subsequent periods) will make possible effective control and direction of all life processes at the levels of biochemistry and of the cell, organism, ecology, and society, from fertility and aging to psychic processes and heredity.

If such an all-encompassing scientific and technological revolution, promising uncounted benefits for mankind, is to be possible and safe, it will require the greatest possible scientific foresight and care and concern for human values of a moral, ethical, and personal character. (I touched briefly on the danger of a thoughtless bureaucratic use of the scientific and technological revolution in a divided world in the section on "Dangers," but could add a great deal more.) Such a revolution will be possible and safe only under highly intelligent worldwide guidance.

The foregoing program presumes:

1. worldwide interest in overcoming the present divisions;

2. the expectation that modifications in both the socialist and capitalist countries will tend to reduce contradictions and differences;

3. worldwide interest of the intelligentsia, the working class, and other progressive forces in a scientific democratic approach to politics, economics, and culture;

4. the absence of insurmountable obstacles to economic development in both world economic systems that might

otherwise lead inevitably into a blind alley, despair, and adventurism.

Every honorable and thinking person who has not been poisoned by narrow-minded indifference will seek to insure that future development will be along the lines of the better alternative. However only broad, open discussion, without the pressure of fear and prejudice, will help the majority to adopt the correct and best course of action.

# A SUMMARY OF PROPOSALS

In conclusion, I will sum up a number of the concrete proposals of varying degrees of importance that have been discussed in the text. These proposals, addressed to the leadership of the country, do not exhaust the content of the
article.

□

The strategy of peaceful coexistence and collaboration
must be deepened in every way. Scientific methods and
principles of international policy will have to be worked
out, based on scientific prediction of the immediate and
more distant consequences.

The initiative must be seized in working out a broad
program of struggle against hunger.

A law on press and information must be drafted, widely

discussed, and adopted, with the aim not only of ending irresponsible and irrational censorship, but also of encouraging self-study in our society, fearless discussion, and the search for truth. The law must provide for the material resources of freedom of thought.

All anti-constitutional laws and decrees violating human rights must be abrogated.

Political prisoners must be amnestied and some of the recent political trials must be reviewed (for example, the Daniel-Sinyavsky and Ginzburg-Galanskov cases). The camp regime of political prisoners must be promptly relaxed.

The exposure of Stalin must be carried through to the end, to the complete truth, and not just to the carefully weighed half truth dictated by caste considerations. The influence of neo-Stalinists in our political life must be restricted in every way (the text mentioned, as an example, the case of S. Trapeznikov, who enjoys too much influence).

The economic reform must be deepened in every way and the area of experimentation expanded, with conclusions based on the results.

A law on geohygiene must be adopted after broad discussion, and ultimately become part of world efforts in this area.

□

With this article the author addresses the leadership of our country and all its citizens as well as all people of goodwill throughout the world. The author is aware of the controversial character of many of his statements. His purpose is open, frank discussion under conditions of publicity.

In conclusion, a textological comment. In the process

of discussion of previous drafts of this article, some incomplete and in some respects one-sided texts have been circulated. Some of them contained certain passages that were inept in form and tact and were included through oversight. The author asks readers to bear this in mind. The author is deeply grateful to readers of preliminary drafts who communicated their friendly comments and thus helped improve the essay and refine a number of basic statements.

*June 1968*

# MANIFESTO II

(AUTHOR'S NOTE: *This was a joint letter and at the present time does not fully express the point of view of at least one of its authors.*)

To the Central Committee of the CPSU, L. I. Brezhnev
To the Council of Ministers of the USSR, A. N. Kosygin
To the Presidium of the Supreme Soviet, N. V. Podgorny

We address ourselves to you on a question having great significance. Our country has achieved a great deal in the development of production, in the fields of education and culture, in the radical improvement of the living conditions of the workers, in the formation of new socialist relations between people. These achievements have worldwide historical importance. They have profoundly influenced events throughout the world and have laid a solid foundation for further successes in the cause of Communism. But we are also faced with serious difficulties and shortcomings.

This letter considers and develops a point of view that briefly can be formulated in the following theses:

□

At the present time it is urgently necessary to carry out a series of measures directed toward the further democratization of public life in the country. This necessity arises from the existence of a close link between the problems of technical-economic progress and scientific methods of management, on the one hand, and questions of information, publicity, and competition on the other. This necessity arises also from other internal and external political problems.

Democratization must facilitate the maintenance and strengthening of the Soviet socialist system, of the socialist economic structure, of our social and cultural achievements and socialist ideology.

Democratization carried out under the direction of the CPSU in cooperation with all levels of society should preserve and strengthen the leading role of the Party in the economic, political, and cultural life of society.

Democratization must be gradual in order to avoid possible complications and disruptions. At the same time, it must be profound and it must be carried out consistently and on the basis of carefully worked-out programs. Without deep-rooted democratization, our society will not be able to solve the problems it faces and will not be able to develop normally.

There is reason to suppose that the point of view expressed in these theses is shared to a greater or lesser extent by a considerable portion of the Soviet intelligentsia and the advanced section of the working class. This point of view finds its reflection in the views of students and working youth and in numerous discussions carried on in private.

However, we consider it appropriate to set forth this point of view in comprehensive written form in order to facilitate, widen, and initiate consideration of important problems. We are seeking to achieve a positive and constructive approach acceptable to the Party-state leadership of the country, and we seek to clarify several misunderstandings and groundless fears.

In the course of the past decade, threatening signs of breakdown and stagnation have been observed in the national economy of our country, although the roots of these difficulties originated in a much earlier period and bear a very profound character. The growth rate of the national income is steadily dropping. There is a widening gap between the requirements for normal development and the real returns from new industrial production. Numerous facts point to errors in determining technical and economic policy in industry and agriculture, as does impermissible red tape in the decision of urgent problems. Defects in the system of planning, accounting, and incentives often lead to a contradiction between local and institutional interests on the one hand and public and state interests on the other. As a result, necessary reserves for the development of production are not available or are not utilized, and technical progress is sharply impeded.

Because of these factors, the natural wealth of the country is frequently destroyed without control and with impunity: forests are cut down; water reservoirs are polluted; valuable agricultural lands are despoiled; soil is eroded and rendered unfit for cultivation; and so forth. It is common knowledge that there is a chronically grave situation in agriculture, especially in livestock. Real income of the population in recent years has hardly risen; nourishment, medical services, and everyday services improve very slowly and unequally between regions. The items of goods in short supply grow. There are obvious signs of inflation. Especially alarming for the future of our country is a slowdown in the development of education. Factually, our general expenditures on education of all types are less than in the United States and are growing more slowly. There is a tragic growth in alcoholism, and narcotics addiction is beginning to make itself felt. In many regions of the country crime is rising systematically, including crime among teenagers and youth. Bureaucracy, compartmentalization, formal attitudes toward jobs, and lack of initiative are growing in the work of scientific and technological organizations.

A decisive factor in the comparison of economic systems is labor productivity. Here the situation is worst of all. Productivity of labor as before remains many times lower than in the developed capitalist countries, and its growth is slowing down. This situation is particularly grave if you compare it with the situation in leading capitalist countries and, in particular, the United States.

By introducing into the economy of the country elements of state regulation and planning these countries have rid themselves of the destructive crises that earlier tore capitalist economies apart. The widespread introduction of automation and computer technology into the economy insures a rapid growth of the productivity of labor, which in turn enables the partial overcoming of severe social diffi-

culties and contradictions (as, for example, ways of establishing unemployment benefits, the shortening of the working day, etc.). Comparing our economy with the economy
of the United States, we see that our economy lags not only
in quantitative but also—which is saddest of all—in qualitative respects.

The newer and more revolutionary the section of the
economy the greater the contrast between the United
States and us. We have exceeded America in coal production but lag in extraction of oil, are ten times behind in natural gas and production of electric power, hopelessly
behind in the chemical field, and immeasurably behind in
computer technology. The last is especially essential, for the
introduction of the computer into the economy is a factor of
decisive importance, radically changing the character of the
system of production and all culture. This phenomenon is
justly called the second industrial revolution. Yet the capacity of our computers is hundreds of times less than that of
the United States, and as regards utilizing computers in the
economy the disparity is so great that it is impossible even
to measure it. We simply live in a different epoch.

The situation is no better in the field of scientific and
engineering discoveries. Here there is no feeling of a growing vitality in our role. On the contrary, at the end of the
1950's our country was the first in the world to launch
Sputniks and send a man into space. At the end of the
1960's we lost our leadership and the first men to land on
the moon were American.

This fact is just one of the external evidences of actual
and growing disparity, on a wide front, of the scientific and
technical level of our country and that of the developed
countries of the West. In the 1920's and 1930's the capitalist

world suffered a period of crises and depression. At that
time we were creating industry at an unbelievable pace, by
employing the enthusiasm of the nation that was a result of
the revolution. At that time our motto was: Catch up with
America and overtake it. And we actually did this for
several decades. Then the situation changed. The second
industrial revolution began. And now, at the beginning of
the 1970's, we can see that we did not catch up with America; we fell behind her more and more.

What is the matter? Why didn't we become the trail-
blazers of the second industrial revolution? Why couldn't
we at least stay even with the most developed capitalist
countries? Is it really true that the socialist system provides
poorer possibilities than the capitalist for the development
of productive force and that in economic competition
socialism can't beat capitalism?

Of course not! The source of our difficulties is not in
the socialist system. On the contrary, it lies in those qualities and conditions of our life that run counter to socialism
and are hostile to it. Their cause—anti-democratic traditions and norms of public life—arose during the Stalin
period and has not been completely liquidated to this day.
Economic constraints, limitations on the exchange of information, restrictions of intellectual freedom, and other
anti-democratic distortions of socialism that took place in
Stalin's time are still accepted as a kind of necessary cost
of the process of industrialization.

It is supposed that these distortions did not affect seriously the country's economy, although they had extremely
serious consequences in the political and military fields, for
the fate of wide strata of the population and whole nationalities. We are leaving aside the problem of how far this

point of view may have been justified regarding the early stages of development of a socialist economy, but the reduced rate of industrial development in the prewar years testifies to the contrary. There is no doubt that with the beginning of the second industrial revolution these phenomena have become the decisive economic factor and the basic obstacle to the development of the country's productive forces.

Due to the increase in the size and complexity of economic systems, problems of organization and management have taken first place. These problems cannot be solved by one individual or even several individuals who possess power and who "know all." They demand the creative participation of millions of people on all levels of the economic system. They demand a wide exchange of information, and this is what distinguishes contemporary economics from, say, the economics of the countries of the ancient East. But in the process of exchanging information and ideas in our country we face insurmountable difficulties. Negative phenomena and real information about our faults are kept secret because they might be "used for hostile propaganda."

The exchange of information with foreign countries is limited by the fear of "penetration of hostile ideology." Theoretical conceptions and practical proposals that seem somehow too bold are suppressed instantly without discussion, out of fear that they may "destroy the foundations."

One can see clear distrust of creative thinkers, critics, and active personalities. Under these conditions those who advance on the service ladder are not those distinguished by high professional qualities and principles but those who by their words display dedication to the cause of the Party, but who in deeds are distinguished only by dedication to their own narrow personal interests or by passive performance.

Restrictions on freedom of information not only make difficult any control over the leadership, not only frustrate the people's initiative, but also deprive even those heading middle-level administrations of both rights and information, transforming them into passive bureaucrats. Our leaders receive incomplete and edited information and are prevented from using their power effectively. The economic reforms of 1965 were extremely useful and an important beginning, calling for the solution of important questions in our economic life. But we are convinced that simple economic measures alone are insufficient for the fulfilling of all these tasks. Moreover, these economic measures cannot be fully undertaken without reforms in the sphere of administration, information, and public knowledge. The same is true of such often-promised initiatives as establishing complex industrial organizations with a high degree of independence in administrative, fiscal, and personnel questions.

It may be concluded that the solution of all economic problems requires a scientific answer to such general and theoretical questions of socialist economics as forms of management feedback, pricing decisions in the absence of a free market, general planning principles, etc.

We are talking a lot now about the necessity of the scientific approach to problems of organization and administration. This, of course, is correct. Only a scientific approach can help overcome difficulties and realize all the possibilities for the direction of the economy and for the technological progress which the absence of capitalist ownership ought to make possible. But the scientific approach requires full information, impartial thinking, and creative freedom. Until these conditions are met (not just for some individuals, but for the masses) the talk about scientific management will remain empty words.

Our economy can be compared with the movement of traffic through an intersection. When there were few cars, traffic police could handle it quite easily and movement was normal. But the number of cars steadily increased. A traffic jam developed. What can be done? The drivers can be fined or the policemen changed. But this will not save the situation. The only way out is to widen the intersection.

The obstacles that prevent the development of our economy can be found outside it, in the political and public area, and all measures that do not eliminate these obstacles will be ineffective.

The consequences of Stalin's period are still negatively affecting the economy, not only directly because of the impossibility of a scientific approach to the problems of administration and management, but also in no less degree indirectly through the general lowering of the creative potential of representatives of all professions.

But it is creative labor that is becoming more and more important for the economy under the conditions of the second industrial revolution. In this connection it is impossible not to speak of the problem of the relationship between the state and the intelligentsia.

Freedom of information and creativity are essential for the intelligentsia because of the nature of its activities and its social function. The desire of the intelligentsia for greater freedom is legitimate and natural. The state, however, suppresses this desire through all kinds of restrictions —administrative pressure, dismissals from work, and even trials. This brings about mutual distrust and profound mutual misunderstanding, which make most difficult any fruitful cooperation between the Party-state structure and the most active—that is, the most socially valuable—strata of the intelligentsia. In conditions of contemporary industrial society, where the role of the intelligentsia is growing continuously, this gap can only be termed suicidal.

Most of the intelligentsia and youth realize the necessity of democratization, the need for cautious and gradual approaches in this matter, but they cannot understand or justify actions having a clearly anti-democratic character. Actually, how can one justify the imprisonment, the detention in camps and psychiatric clinics, of persons who are oppositionists but whose opposition is still within legal bounds in the area of ideas and convictions? In a series of cases the matter lies not in some kind of opposition, but in a simple desire for information, for frank, impartial discussion of important social questions!

It is impermissible to keep writers in prison because of their work. One cannot understand or justify such stupid, harmful measures as the expulsion from the Writers Union of the greatest and most popular Soviet writer [Alexander Solzhenitsyn], nor the destruction of the editorial board of *Novy Mir,* around which gathered the most progressive forces of Marxist-Leninist socialist direction!

One must speak again of ideological problems.

Democratization with full information and competition must return to our ideological life (social science, art, propaganda) its essential dynamism and creative character, liquidating the bureaucratic, ritualistic, dogmatic, official-hypocritical ungifted style that today occupies so important a place.

A policy of democratization would remove the gap between the Party-state apparatus and the intelligentsia. Mutual lack of understanding would be replaced by close cooperation. A policy of democratization would stimulate enthusiasm comparable to that of the 1920's. The best intellectual forces of the country would be mobilized for the solution of social and economic problems.

To carry out democratization is not easy. Its normal progress will be threatened from one side by individualist, anti-socialist forces and from the other side by those worshipers of "strong power," demagogues of a fascist type who may attempt to utilize the economic difficulties of the country for their own aims, and by mutual misunderstanding and mistrust on the part of the intelligentsia and the Party-state apparatus and the existence in some levels of society of bourgeois and nationalist sentiments.

But we must realize that there is no other way out for our country and that this difficult problem must be solved. Democratization at the initiative of, and under the control of, the highest authorities will allow this process to advance gradually and thus to enable all the links of the Party-state apparatus successfully to change over to the new style of work, which, in contrast with the past, will involve greater public information, openness, and wider discussion of all problems.

There is no doubt that the majority of officials, who are, of course, people educated in a contemporary, highly developed country, are capable of adapting to this style of work and very quickly will feel its advantages. The comparatively small number unable to do so will leave the apparatus—to its advantage. We propose the following tentative measures that could be carried out in the course of four or five years:

□

A statement by the highest party and government organs on the necessity of further democratization, on the tempo and method of achieving it; publication in the press of a number of articles discussing the problems of democratization.

Restricted distribution (through Party and state organs, organizations, and institutions) of information on the state of the country and theoretical work on public problems, which for the time being should not be made a subject of wide discussion. Gradual increase in circulation of such material until it is fully available to everyone.

Widespread organization of industrial establishments with a high degree of independence in questions of industrial planning and production processes, sales and supplies, finances, and personnel, and widening these privileges for smaller units. Scientific determination after careful research of the forms and extent of state regulation.

An end to jamming foreign broadcasts. Free sale of foreign books and periodicals. Accession of our country to the international copyright system. Gradual (over three to four years) expansion and easing of international tourism on both sides. Freer international correspondence and other measures for the expansion of international contacts, particularly in relation to the Comecon countries.

Establishment of an institute for the study of public opinion, restricted at first and then with complete publication of materials, showing the attitude of the population to the most important problems of internal and foreign policy and also other sociological material.

Amnesty for political prisoners. A decree on compulsory publication of full stenographic records of trials of a political nature. Public control over places of imprisonment and over psychiatric institutions.

[The number of political prisoners is not great compared to the Stalin days but totals, by a conservative estimate, several thousand.]

Institution of other measures to improve the work of courts and procurators' offices, and to establish their independence from the executive power, local influence, prejudice, and connections.

Elimination of the nationality designation in passports. A single system of passports for urban and rural areas. Gradual elimination of passport registration, carried out simultaneously with elimination of inequities in regional economic and cultural development.

[Every Soviet citizen must possess an "internal" passport for travel, work, and life within his country. Each passport carries a designation of his "nationality" (Russian, Ukrainian, Uzbek, Jewish, etc.).]

Reforms in the field of education. Greater appropriations for primary and secondary schools, improvement of the material situation of teachers, giving them greater independence and the right to experiment.

Passage of a law on the press and information facilitating the possibility of creating new publishers by public organizations and groups of citizens.

Improvement of the training of leading cadres versed in the art of management. Introduction of practical training for managers. Improvement of the knowledgeability of leadership cadres at all levels, their rights to independence, to experimentation, and to the defense of their opinions and the testing of them in practice.

Gradual introduction into practice of the nomination of several candidates for each office in elections for Party and government organs at all levels, including indirect elections.

Widening the rights of Soviet organs. Widening the rights and responsibilities of the Supreme Soviet of the USSR.

Restoration of the rights of all nations forcibly resettled under Stalin. Restoration of the national autonomy of the resettled peoples. Granting them the possibility of resettling in former homelands (where this has not already been done).

Measures designed to increase public disclosure of the work of the leading organs within limits determined by state interests. Creation of committees composed of highly qualified scientists from different specialties to consult with leading organs at all levels.

☐

Of course this plan must be regarded as approximate. It is also clear that it must be supplemented by a plan for economic and social measures worked out by specialists. We emphasize that democratization in itself does not solve economic problems. It only creates preconditions for their solution. But without creation of these preconditions, economic problems cannot be solved. Sometimes we hear our foreign friends comparing the Soviet Union to a powerful truck, whose driver is pressing on the gas with one foot as hard as possible while stepping on the brake at the same time. The time has come to use the brake more sensibly.

The plan we propose shows, in our view, that it is quite possible to outline a program of democratization that is acceptable to the Party and the state and satisfies, as a first approximation, the urgent demands of the nation's development. Naturally, wide discussion, profound scientific, sociological, economic, political, pedagogic, and other research, as well as actual practice, will provide essential corrections and additions. But it is important, as the mathematicians say, to prove "the theorem of the existence of a solution."

We must also consider the international consequences of democratization if it is adopted by our country. Nothing can so well serve our international authority and strengthen progressive Communist forces in the entire world as further democratization, accompanied by an intensification of the technological and economic progress of the world's first socialist country. Doubtless possibilities will increase for peaceful coexistence and international cooperation; the forces of peace and social progress will be strengthened; the attractiveness of Communist ideology will grow; and our international position will become more secure. Particularly vital is the fact that our moral and material position relative to China will be strengthened, making it possible (indirectly, by example of technical aid) to influence the situation in that country in the interests of the peoples of both countries.

A number of correct and necessary foreign policy actions by our government are not properly understood because the information provided to citizens on these matters is incomplete, and in the past there have been cases of plain inaccuracy and tendentious information, which increase the lack of confidence.

One example is the question of economic aid to underdeveloped countries. Fifty years ago the workers of Europe, ravaged by war, helped those dying of hunger in the Volga region. Soviet people today are not callous or egotistical. But they must be sure that our resources are being spent on real aid, on the solution of serious problems, not on the construction of grandiose stadiums and for the purchase of

American cars for local bureaucrats. The situation in the modern world and the opportunities and tasks facing our country demand wide participation in economic aid to the underdeveloped nations in cooperation with other countries. But for a correct understanding of these questions on the part of the public it is not enough to give verbal assurances. Proofs must be given and needs must be shown, and this demands fuller information and democratization.

Soviet foreign policy, in its basic features, is a policy of peace and cooperation.

The public's lack of information causes disquiet. In the past there occurred certain negative phenomena in Soviet foreign policy, which had the character of excessive ambitiousness, messianism, and which force one to the conclusion that it is not only the imperialists who bear the responsibility for international tension. All negative phenomena in our foreign policy are closely connected with the problem of democratization, and this works both ways. Great disquiet is caused by the absence of democratic discussion of such questions as arms aid to a number of countries, including, for instance, Nigeria, where a bloody civil war was in progress whose causes and course were quite unfamiliar to the Soviet public. We are convinced that the resolution of the United Nations Security Council on the problems of the Arab-Israeli conflict is just and reasonable, although it is not definite enough in a number of important points. However, disquiet is caused by the question: Does our position not go substantially further than this document? Is it not too one-sided? Is it always realistic for us to strive to extend our influence in places far from our borders in a time of difficulties in Sino-Soviet relations and in technological and economic development?

Of course in certain cases such a "dynamic policy" is essential, but it must be harmonized not only with general principles but also with the nation's real capabilities. We are convinced that the only realistic policy in an age of thermonuclear weapons is a course aimed at a continued deepening of international cooperation, at determined attempts to find a line of possible convergence in scientific, technological, economic, cultural, and ideological spheres, and the renunciation of weapons of mass destruction as a matter of principle.

We take this opportunity to support unilateral and joint declarations of principle by nuclear powers renouncing the first use of mass-destruction weapons.

Democratization will facilitate a better public understanding of our foreign policy and remove from it all its negative features. This in turn will lead to the disappearance of one of the chief "trumps" held by the opponents of democratization. Another of their "trumps"—the well-known mutual lack of understanding between government-Party circles and the intelligentsia—will disappear at the very first stages of democratization.

□

What awaits our country if a course toward democratization is not taken? We will fall behind the capitalist countries in the course of the second industrial revolution and be gradually transformed into a second-rate provincial power (history has known similar examples); economic difficulties will increase; relations between the Party-state apparatus and the intelligentsia will deteriorate, with dangerous clashes between right and left; and nationality problems will be exacerbated, for in the national republics the movement for democratization, arising from below, inevitably takes on a nationalistic character. The prospect becomes particularly menacing if one takes into consideration the presence of a danger from Chinese totalitarian nationalism (which in a historical context we regard as temporary but very serious in the coming years). We can counter this danger only if we increase or at least maintain the technological and economic gap between our country and China, if we add to the number of our friends in the world at large, and if we offer the Chinese people the alternative of cooperation and aid. This becomes obvious if one takes into consideration the numerical superiority of the potential enemy and his militant nationalism, as well as the great extent of our eastern frontiers and the sparse population of the eastern regions.

Thus, economic stagnation, which slows up the rate of development, in combination with an insufficiently realistic and sometimes too ambitious foreign policy on all continents may lead our country to catastrophic consequences.

□

Respected Comrades:

There is no way out of the difficulties facing the country except a course toward democratization carried out by the Party in accordance with a carefully worked out program. A move to the right, that is, the victory of the tendency toward harsh administrative measures and "tightening the screws," will not solve any problems; on the contrary, it will aggravate those problems to the extreme and lead the country into a tragic blind alley. The tactics of passively waiting to see what happens will lead in the final analysis to the same result. Presently we have a chance to take the right road and carry out the necessary reforms. In a few years, perhaps, it will be too late. This problem must be recognized by the whole country.

It is the duty of everyone who sees the source of the difficulties and the means of overcoming them to point this out to his fellow citizens. Understanding the need and opportunity for a gradual democratization is the first step on the road to its realization.

A. D. SAKHAROV
V. F. TURCHIN
R. A. MEDVEDEV

*March 19, 1970*

[The following footnote was attached to the letter:]

On January 8, 1970, a "letter to L. I. Brezhnev" was widely distributed in Moscow, signed by the name "Sakarov" or "Academician Sakarov." This "letter" in several variations was published subsequently in the foreign press. In issue No. 1 for 1970 of the anti-Soviet emigré journal Possev was published an article under the pretentious title "The Truth about Contemporary Times" over the signature of "R. Medvedev." This article, a complete fabrication, was broadcast subsequently in the Russian language by Radio Liberty (FRG). We declare we are not the authors of the forementioned letter and article. These documents present us in a completely false light and are evidently distributed with provocational aims. Signed:

R. A. MEDVEDEV
A. D. SAKHAROV

# MEMORANDUM

I request a discussion of the general questions partially discussed in a previous letter from R. A. Medvedev, V. F. Turchin, and myself, and in my letter of 1968. I also request the consideration of a number of particular questions of a topical nature that I find extremely disturbing.

I have included below, in two general lists, questions that, although differing in degree of importance and self-evidence, have a definite inner connection. A discussion and partial argumentation of these questions will be found in the above-mentioned letters and in the postscript to this memorandum.

I wish also to inform you that in November 1970, I, together with V. N. Chalidze and A. N. Tverdokhlebov, was involved in the creation of a "Human Rights Committee" for the purpose of studying the problem of safeguarding

human rights and promoting the growth of a legal awareness. I enclose some of the committee's documents. We
hope to be useful to society, and we seek a dialogue with
the country's leadership and a frank and public discussion of problems of human rights.

# SOME URGENT PROBLEMS

The problems listed below appear to me to need urgent consideration.

For brevity's sake they have been expressed in the form of proposals. While recognizing that some of these problems require further study, and conscious that the list is of necessity an incomplete and therefore to a certain extent a subjective one (I have tried to set out several equally important questions in the second half of this memorandum, while several could not be included at all), I nevertheless consider that a discussion of the following proposals by the competent authorities is essential.

*1. Concerning political persecution.* I feel it is high time to consider the pressing problem of implementing a general amnesty for political prisoners, that is, persons convicted under Articles 70, 72, 190–1, –2 and –3 of the RSFSR

Criminal Code and the equivalent articles of the codes of
the union republics; persons convicted on religious grounds;
persons confined in psychiatric institutions; persons sentenced for attempting to cross the frontier; and political
prisoners given an additional sentence for attempting to
escape or for disseminating propaganda in their camp.

Measures should be taken to insure real and widespread public access to the hearings of all legal proceedings, especially those of a political character. I consider it
important that all judicial verdicts carried in violation of
the principle of public access should be reviewed.

I hold inadmissible all psychiatric [methods of] repression on political, ideological, and religious grounds. I am
of the opinion that a law must be passed to protect the
rights of persons subjected to compulsory psychiatric hospitalization; resolutions must be passed and the necessary
legislative measures introduced to protect the rights of persons assumed to be mentally ill in the course of a prosecution on political charges. In particular, private psychiatric
investigation by commissions independent of the authorities should be allowed in both cases.

Independently of the general solution of these problems, I request the examination by the competent organs of
a number of pressing individual cases, some of which are
listed in the attached note.

2. *Concerning publicity, freedom of information exchange, and freedom of beliefs.* A bill concerning the press
and the mass media should be submitted for nationwide
discussion.

A resolution should be passed calling for greater freedom in the publication of statistical and sociological data.

3. *Concerning nationalities problems and the problem*

*of leaving the country.* Resolutions and laws should be passed fully restoring the rights of peoples deported under Stalin.

Laws should be passed to insure that citizens may easily and without hindrance exercise their right to leave the country and freely return to it. The directives restricting this right and in contravention of the law should be annulled.

4. *Concerning international problems.* We should show initiative and announce (or affirm, unilaterally at first) our refusal to be the first to use weapons of mass destruction (nuclear, chemical, bacteriological, and incendiary weapons). We should allow inspection teams to visit our territory for effective arms control (assuming that we conclude an agreement on disarmament or partial limitation of certain types of armaments).

In order to consolidate the results of our changed relations with East Germany we should work out a new, more flexible, and realistic position on the question of West Berlin.

We should alter our political position in the Middle East and in Vietnam, and actively seek, through the United Nations and diplomatic channels, a peaceful settlement in the shortest possible time, on the basis of a compromise, with the renunciation by the United States and the USSR of any intervention, military or political, direct or indirect; the promotion of a program of large-scale economic aid on an apolitical, international basis (through the United Nations?); and the proposal that UN troops be widely used to safeguard political and military stability in these areas.

# THESES AND PROPOSALS WITH REGARD TO GENERAL PROBLEMS

By way of preparation for a discussion of the basic problems of the development and foreign policy of our country I have attempted to formulate a number of theses. Some of them are set out in the form of discussion points. I have tried to give the fullest possible exposition of my views, although I realize that some of the theses will seem unacceptable and others uninteresting or insignificant.

1. Since the year 1950 a number of important measures have been taken in our country to eliminate the most dangerous and ugly features of the previous stage of development of Soviet society and state policies. However, at the same time there do occur certain negative phenomena—deviations, inconsistencies, and sluggishness in the implementation of the new line. It is essential to work out a clear-cut and consistent program of further democratization and

liberalization, and to take a number of immediate steps as a matter of urgency. This is required in the interests of technical and economic progress, of gradually overcoming our backwardness and isolation from the advanced capitalist countries, and [in the interests of] the prosperity of large sectors of the population, internal stability, and external security. The development of our country is taking place in the extremely difficult conditions presented by our relations with China. We are faced with serious internal difficulties in the sphere of the economy and the general standard of living, technical and economic progress, culture and ideology.

One must point out the increasingly acute nationalities problem, the complexities of the interrelationship between the Party-state apparatus and the intelligentsia, and of that between the basic mass of the workers, who find themselves relatively worse off with regard to their standard of living and financial status, their prospects for professional promotion and cultural development, and many of whom feel disillusioned with all the "fine words," and the privileged group of "the bosses," whom the more backward sectors of the workers frequently, and chiefly by virtue of traditional prejudices, identify with the intelligentsia. Our country's foreign policy is not always sufficiently realistic. We need basic decisions in order to prevent possible complications.

2. I venture the opinion that it would be correct to characterize as follows the society toward the creation of which urgent state reforms as well as the efforts of citizens to develop a social conscience should be directed:

The basic aim of the state is the protection and safeguarding of the basic rights of its citizens. The defense of human rights is the loftiest of all aims.

State institutions always act in complete accordance with laws (which are stable, and known to all citizens, institutions, and organizations).

The happiness of the people is safeguarded, in particular, by their freedom of work, freedom of consumption, freedom in their private lives, and in their education, their cultural and their social activities, freedom of conviction and of conscience, and freedom of exchange of information, and of movement.

Openness facilitates the social controls safeguarding legality, justice, and the rightness of all decisions taken, contributes to the effectiveness of the entire system, makes for a scientific and democratic system of government, and promotes progress, prosperity, and national security.

Competitiveness, openness, and the absence of privileges insure an equitable distribution of incentives for the labor, personal capabilities, and individual initiative of all citizens.

There is a definite stratification of society based on type of occupation, nature of abilities, and [social] relations.

The basic energies of the country are directed toward harmonious internal development, with the purposeful deployment of labor and natural resources, and this is the basis of its power and prosperity. The country and its people are always ready to enter into friendly international cooperation and aid within the framework of universal brotherhood, but the society is such that it does not need to use foreign policy as a means of internal political stabilization, or to extend its spheres of influence, or to export its ideas. Messianism, delusions as to the uniqueness of a society and the exclusive merits of its own path, as well as the rejection of the paths of other [societies], are alien to [the ideal] society; organically alien to it also are dogmatism, adventurism, and aggression.

In the actual conditions obtaining in our country in particular, we will only overcome our economic difficulties and improve the people's standard of living by a concentration of resources on internal problems, and, given some additional conditions (democratization, the elimination of our people's isolation in terms of access to information from the rest of the world, and economic measures), this alone will give us any hope of gradually narrowing the gap between ourselves and the advanced capitalist countries, safeguard national security in the event of a deterioration in [our relations with] China, and insure that we have ample opportunity to assist countries in need.

3. *Foreign policy.* Our chief foreign policy problem is our relations with China. While offering the Chinese people the alternative of economic, technical, and cultural aid, and fraternal cooperation and progress together along the road of democracy, and always leaving open the possibility of developing relations in this way, we must at the same time display a special concern for the safeguarding of our national security, avoid all other possible complications in our foreign and domestic policies, and implement our plans for the development of Siberia, keeping this element in mind.

We must aim at noninterference in the internal affairs of other socialist countries, and mutual economic aid.

We must take the initiative in calling for the creation (within the framework of the United Nations?) of a new international consultative organ, an "International Council of Experts on the Problems of Peace, Disarmament, Economic Aid to Needy Countries, the Defense of Human

Rights, and the Protection of the Environment," consisting of authoritative and impartial individuals. The council's statutes, and the procedure for the election of its members, must guarantee it maximum independence of the interests of individual states and groups of states. In deciding the composition and statutes of the council, it is probably essential to take into account the wishes of the main international organizations. An international pact must be signed obliging legislative and governmental organs to examine the "council of experts" recommendations, which must be well founded and open to scrutiny. The decisions of national organs with regard to these recommendations must be openly proclaimed, irrespective of whether the recommendations are accepted or rejected.

4. *Economic problems, management, personnel.* Extension of the 1965 economic reform, increase in the economic independence of all units of production, review of a number of restrictive regulations with regard to the selection of personnel, salaries and incentives, systems of material supply and stocks, planning, cooperation, choice of output profile, and allocation of funds.

Management and personnel: resolutions should be passed to make the work of state institutions at all levels more open to public scrutiny, as far as the interests of the state will allow. A review of the "behind-closed-doors" tradition is especially vital. With regard to the problems of personnel policy, there should be increased open and active public control over the selection of personnel and there should be procedures for the election of management personnel at all levels and their replacement if they are found unsuitable. I also suggest the normal requirement of any democratic program: the system of holding elections in the absence of a number of candidates, that is, "election without choice," must be abolished. At the same time the following are essential: increased availability of information; self-sufficiency; the right to experiment; a shift in the center of responsibility toward the subsidiary enterprise and its employees; improved methods of specialist instruction and business training for management personnel at all levels; the abolition of special privileges linked with professional and Party ranking, since these are very harmful in social and working relations; publication of official salaries; reorganization of personnel departments; abolition of the system of *nomenklatura* and other such survivals of the previous epoch; the creation of scientific-consultative councils attached to authorities, to be composed of scholars with various specialist qualifications, and endowed with the necessary independence.

Measures to promote the expansion of agricultural production on private plots belonging to collective farmers, workers on state farms, and individual peasants; changes in fiscal policy; increased land usage in the agricultural sector; changes in the system of supplying this sector with modern, purpose-built agricultural machinery, fertilizers, etc. Measures to improve the supply of building materials and fuel to the village; the expansion of all forms of cooperative farming in the village, with changes in fiscal policy, permission to hire and pay laborers in accordance with the requirements of the job, and changes in the system of supplying materials to the village.

Increased opportunity for and profitability of private initiative in the service industries, health service, small trading, education, and so on.

5. The question of the gradual abolition of the pass-

port regulations should be examined, since these are a serious hindrance to the development of the country's productive resources and a violation of civil rights, particularly those of rural dwellers.

6. *Information exchange, culture, science, and freedom of beliefs.* Freedom of beliefs, the spirit of inquiry, and creative anxiety should be encouraged.

The jamming of foreign radio broadcasts should be stopped, more foreign literature brought in from abroad, the international copyright agreement signed, and foreign travel facilitated, in order to overcome the isolation that is having a pernicious effect on our development.

Resolutions should be passed insuring the real separation of church and state, and real (that is, legally, economically, and administratively guaranteed) freedom of conscience and worship.

A review should be carried out of those aspects of the interrelations between the Party-state apparatus and art, literature, theater, organs of education, and so on that are harmful to the development of culture in our country, reduce the boldness and versatility of the creative endeavor, and lead to conventionality, grayness, and ritual repetition. In the social sciences and the humanities, which play an ever greater role in modern life (philosophy, history, sociology, jurisprudence, etc.), we must insure the elimination of stagnation, a widening of scope in the creative endeavor, an independence of all superimposed opinions, and the use of the entire gamut of foreign experience.

7. *Social policies.* The possibility of abolishing the death penalty should be explored. Special- and strict-regime imprisonment should be abolished, since it conflicts with humaneness. Measures should be taken to perfect the

penitentiary system, utilizing foreign experience and the recommendations of the UN.

A study should be made of the possibility of setting up a public supervisory organ to eliminate the use of physical coercion (assault, starvation, cold, etc.) against detainees, persons under arrest or investigation, and convicted persons.

There must be a radical improvement in the quality of education: increased salaries and independence for schoolteachers and college lecturers should be given; less importance should be attached to the formal role of diplomas and degrees; the educational system should be less monolithic; a wider range of subjects should be studied in schools; there should be increased guarantees of the right of freedom of beliefs.

Intensified measures should be taken in the struggle against alcoholism, including the possibility of public control over all aspects of the problem.

Stronger measures should be implemented in the struggle against noise, air and water pollution, erosion, the salting and chemical pollution of the soil. More should be done to preserve forests and wild and domestic animals, as well as to prevent cruelty to animals.

Reform of the health service, expansion of the network of private polyclinics and hospitals; a more important role for doctors, nurses, and health visitors in private practice; salary increases for health-service employees at all levels; reform of the drug industry; general access to modern medicines and equipment; the introduction of X-ray television equipment.

8. *Legal policies.* All forms of discrimination, overt and concealed, with regard to beliefs, national characteristics, etc., should be abolished.

There should be real openness of legal proceedings, wherever this does not conflict with basic civil rights.

What should be taken up again is the question of the ratification by the USSR Supreme Soviet of the pacts on human rights concluded at the Twenty-first Session of the UN General Assembly, and of [the USSR's] signing the optional protocol to these pacts.

9. *Interrelations with the national republics.* Our country has proclaimed the right of a nation to self-determination, even if this means secession. In the case of Finland, implementation of the right to secede was sanctioned by the Soviet government. The right of union republics to secede is proclaimed by the USSR Constitution. There is, however, some vagueness in the relationship between these guarantees and the procedures regarding preparation for, necessary discussion of, and actual implementation of this right. In fact, the mere discussion of such questions frequently leads to prosecution. In my opinion, a juridical settlement of the problem and the passing of a law guaranteeing the right to secession would be of great internal and international significance as a confirmation of the anti-imperialist and anti-chauvinist nature of our policies. The number of republics tending toward secession is, to all appearances, very small, and these tendencies would doubtless become even weaker with time as a result of the future democratization of the USSR. On the other hand, there can be no doubt that any republic that secedes from the USSR for one reason or another by peaceful, constitutional means would maintain intact its ties with the socialist commonwealth of nations. In this case, the economic interests and defense capabilities of the socialist camp would not suffer, since the cooperation of the socialist countries is by nature complete and all-embracing and will doubtless become

even more extensive in conditions of mutual noninterference in each other's internal affairs. For these reasons, discussion of the question I have raised does not seem to me to be dangerous.

☐

If this memorandum appears here and there to be excessively peremptory in tone, that must be put down to its abbreviated form. The problems with which our country is confronted are closely connected with some aspects of the general world crisis of the twentieth century—the crisis of international security, of loss of stability in social development, the ideological impasse and disillusionment with the ideals of the recent past, nationalism, and the threat of dehumanization. The constructive, prudent, flexible, and at the same time decisive solution of our problems will, by virtue of our country's special position in the world, be of tremendous significance for the whole of mankind.

*March 5, 1971*

# POSTSCRIPT
# TO
# MEMORANDUM

*The "Memorandum" was sent to the Secretary General of the CPSU [Mr. Brezhnev] on March 5, 1971. It received no reply. I do not think it would be right for me to delay its publication any longer. The "Postscript" was written in June 1972. It contains some additions to and partly replaces the note "Concerning political persecution" mentioned in the text.*

I began my activity approximately ten to twelve years ago, when I realized the criminal character of a possible thermonuclear war and of thermonuclear tests in the atmosphere. Since then I have revised my views to a considerable extent, particularly since the year 1968, which began for me with work on *Progress, Coexistence, and Intellectual Freedom,* and ended, as for everybody else, with the rumbling of tanks in the streets of unyielding Prague.

As before, I cannot fail to appreciate the great and

beneficial changes (social, cultural, and economic) that have taken place in our country in the last fifty years, realizing, however, that analogous changes have taken place in many countries and that they are a manifestation of worldwide progress.

As before, I consider that it will be possible to overcome the tragic conflicts and dangers of our time only through the convergence of capitalism and the socialist regime.

In capitalist countries this process must be accompanied by a further improvement in the protection of workers' rights and a reduction in the role of militarism and its influence on political life. In socialist countries it is also essential to reduce the militarization of the economy and the role of a messianic ideology. It is vitally necessary to weaken the extreme forms of centralism and Party-state bureaucratic monopoly, both in the economic sphere of production and consumption, and in the sphere of ideology and culture.

As before, I consider the democratization of society, the development of openness in public affairs, the rule of law, and the safeguarding of basic human rights to be of decisive importance.

As before, I hope that society will evolve along these lines under the influence of technological-economic progress, although my prognoses have now become more cautious.

It seems to me now, more than ever before, that the only true guarantee for the safeguarding of human values in the chaos of uncontrollable changes and tragic upheavals is man's freedom of conscience and his moral yearning for the good.

Our society is infected by apathy, hypocrisy, petit

bourgeois egoism, and hidden cruelty. The majority of representatives of its upper stratum—the Party apparatus of government and the highest, most successful layers of the intelligentsia—cling tenaciously to their open and secret privileges and are profoundly indifferent to the infringement of human rights, the interests of progress, security, and the future of mankind. Others, though deeply concerned in their hearts, cannot allow themselves any freedom of thought and are condemned to the torture of internal conflict. Drunkenness has assumed the dimensions of a national calamity. It is one of the symptoms of the moral degradation of a society that is sinking ever deeper into a state of chronic alcoholic poisoning.

The country's spiritual regeneration demands the elimination of those conditions that drive people into becoming hypocritical and time-serving, and that lead to feelings of impotence, discontent, and disillusionment. Everybody must be assured, in deed and not just in word, of equal opportunities for advancement in his work, in education, and cultural growth; and the system of privileges in all spheres of consumption must be abolished. Full intellectual freedom must be assured and all forms of persecution for beliefs must cease. A radical educational reform is essential. These ideas are the basis of many proposals in the memorandum.

In particular, the memorandum mentions the problem of improvement in the material condition and independence of two of the most numerous and socially significant groups of the intelligentsia, the teachers and medical workers. The sorry state of popular education and of the health service is carefully hidden from the eyes of foreigners, but cannot remain secret from those who wish to see.

A free health service and education are no more than an economic illusion in a society in which all surplus value is expropriated and distributed by the state. The hierarchical class structure of our society, with its system of privileges, is reflected in a particularly pernicious way in the health service and education. The condition of the health service and of popular education is clearly revealed in the rundown state of public hospitals, in the poverty of the village schools, with their overcrowded classes, the poverty and low standing of the teacher, and the official hypocrisy in teaching, which inculcates in the rising generation a spirit of indifference toward moral, artistic, and scientific values.

The most essential condition for the cure of our society is the abandonment of political persecution, in its judicial and psychiatric forms or in any other form of which our bureaucratic and bigoted system, with its totalitarian interference by the state in the lives of the citizens, is capable, such as dismissal from work, expulsion from college, refusal of residence permits, limitation of promotion at work, etc.

The first beginnings of a moral regeneration of the people and the intelligentsia, which resulted from the curbing of the most extreme manifestations of the Stalinist system of blind terror, met with no proper understanding in ruling circles. The basic class, social, and ideological features of the regime did not undergo any essential change. With pain and alarm I have to note that after a period of largely illusory liberalism there is once again an extension of restrictions on ideological freedom, efforts to suppress information not controlled by the state, fresh persecution for political and ideological reasons, and a deliberate aggravation of nationalities problems. The fifteen months since the submission of the memorandum have brought new and disturbing evidence about the development of these tendencies.

The wave of political arrests in the first few months of 1972 is particularly alarming. Numerous arrests took place in the Ukraine. Arrests have also taken place in Moscow, Leningrad, and other regions of the country.

The attention of the public has also been drawn during these months to the trial of Bukovsky in Moscow and of Strokatova in Odessa, and other trials. The use of psychiatry for political purposes is fraught with extremely dangerous consequences for society and constitutes a completely inadmissible interference with basic human rights. There have been numerous protests and pronouncements on this question. At present Grigorenko, Gershuni, and many others are being kept in prison-type psychiatric hospitals, the fate of Fainberg and Borisov is unknown; there are other instances of psychiatric repression (e.g., the case of the poet Lupynis in the Ukraine).

The persecution and destruction of religion, which has been carried on with perseverance and cruelty for decades, has resulted in what is undoubtedly one of the most serious infringements of the rights of man in our country. Freedom of religious belief and activity is an integral part of intellectual freedom as a whole. Unfortunately, the last few months have been marked by fresh instances of religious persecution, in particular in the Baltic states.

In this postscript I am passing over a series of important problems that were dealt with in the memorandum and my other published documents—in the open letter to the members of the Presidium of the Supreme Soviet of the USSR, "On freedom to leave the country," and to the Minister of Internal Affairs, "On discrimination against the Crimean Tatars."

I also pass over the majority of international problems dealt with in the memorandum. I will single out from their number the question of arms race limitations. Militarization of the economy leaves a deep imprint on international and domestic policy; it leads to encroachment on democratic rights, the open conduct of public affairs, and the rule of law; it constitutes a threat to peace. The role of the military-industrial complex in United States policy has been thoroughly studied. The analogous role played by the same factors in the USSR and other socialist countries is less well known. It is, however, necessary to point out that in no country does the share of military expenditure with relation to the national income reach such proportions as in the USSR (over 40 percent). In an atmosphere of mutual suspicion the problem of control mentioned in the memorandum assumes a special role.

I write this postscript a short time after the signing of important agreements on the limitation of ABM and strategic missiles. One would like to believe that political leaders and the people who are active in the military-industrial complexes of the United States and the USSR have a sense of responsibility toward humanity.

One would like to believe that these agreements are not merely of symbolic importance, but will lead to a real curtailment of the arms race and to further steps that would improve the political climate in our long-suffering world.

In conclusion, I consider it necessary to emphasize in particular the importance I attach to the proposal for the setting up of an international consultative committee, "The International Council of Experts," which would have the right to put forward recommendations to national governments that they would be obliged to consider (3. under Theses and Proposals with Regard to General Problems, in the memorandum). I think this proposal is feasible if it receives the wide international support for which I appeal, and I appeal not only to Soviet but also to foreign readers. I hope too that my voice from "inside" the socialist world may contribute in some measure to the understanding of the historical experience of the last decade.

*June 1972*

# LET SOVIET CITIZENS EMIGRATE

The trials of recent months have once again reminded us of the tragic conflicts faced by Soviet citizens who wish to emigrate and resettle in another country as well as the legal, social, psychological, and political aspects of this problem.

Soviet citizens, both Jews and those of other nationalities—Russians, Ukrainians, Germans, Armenians, Lithuanians, Latvians, Estonians, Meskhi Turks, and others—who have sought to leave for personal, ethnic, and other reasons have found their lives transformed into constant torture by years of expectation only to receive unjustified refusals.

There is another side to this problem. Concern can only be caused by the fate of those who, having lost hope of satisfying their aspirations within the framework of the law, decided to break the law in one way or another.

Many of these people have been sentenced to long terms of detention in camps or prisons or have been doomed to the horror of forced psychiatric treatment in such strict-regimen hospitals as the Dnepropetrovsk special psychiatric hospital and others.

The attempts made by these citizens, prompted by extreme necessity, have for the most part been categorized by the courts as betrayal of the Motherland, and have resulted in most severe punishment.

In December 1970, the world was stunned by the sentences in the so-called Leningrad case about an attempted hijacking. Two death sentences were commuted by an appeals court, but the public punishment remained exceptionally strict for the sentenced.

In May 1971, a Lithuanian, Simas Kudirka, whose only guilt was an attempt to remain abroad during a voyage overseas, was sentenced to ten years' detention by a court in Vilna. He was able to jump onto an American warship, but was returned and sentenced for "betrayal of the Motherland."

From a legal viewpoint these trials are similar to one that took place in August 1971 at which the physicist Dmitri Mikheev was sentenced to eight years' detention for attempting to leave the country and exchanging documents with a foreigner, François de Perrego, a Swiss citizen. The latter was sentenced to three years.

Finally, there is yet another side to the problem. Persons attempting to leave, usually without success, find themselves in doing so in the position of second-class citizens with regard to retaining a number of their rights—because of prejudices, traditions, and conformism in our society.

This involves the opportunity of continuing with one's studies or with one's job, and may even result in judicial prosecution. The recent trials of Palatnik in Odessa and Kukui in Sverdlovsk are, in my opinion, examples of such preconceived and obviously unjust approaches.

Commenting on the above aspects of the problem as a whole, I would like to stress that a humane and just solution would be highly important to further democratization of our country, for the final overcoming of our international isolation, for an exchange of people and ideas, and for the defense of the rights of man—that primary and basic value of a socio-political system.

· The freedom to emigrate, which only a small number of people would in fact use, is an essential condition of spiritual freedom. A free country cannot resemble a cage, even if it is gilded and supplied with material things.

Respected members of the Supreme Soviet, I appeal to you, I appeal to anyone who wants the citizens of this country to be truly free, to contribute in every way possible to a solution of these problems. In particular, I appeal to you personally to take the initiative in the following:

It is essential to adopt legislation that would resolve the problem of emigration in a democratic spirit so that anyone who desires to leave the country will be given the opportunity to do so and, if he then changes his mind, to return home without hindrance. This would be in keeping with the rights of man that are universally acknowledged.

Further, it is essential that the section of the criminal code on high treason be amended so that it will no longer be interpreted as broadly as has been evident in recent trial practice.

It is essential to grant amnesty to all citizens sentenced

in connection with attempts to leave the country and to release those who, for the same reason, are being subjected to forced treatment in special psychiatric hospitals.

*October 7, 1971*

# INTERVIEW WITH OLLE STENHOLM, SWEDISH RADIO CORRESPONDENT

. . . The most natural thing for anyone in this situation is to regard his system as the best. Thus, any deviation from this view is already some kind of a psychological process. And when in 1968 I wrote my work [*Progress, Coexistence, and Intellectual Freedom*] this process was still in its beginning stages and my own approach was more abstract. My life has been such that I began by confronting global problems and only later on more concrete, personal, and human ones. Thus, in evaluating my essay of 1968 you must understand this and take into account the route I followed from work on thermonuclear weapons to my concern about the results of nuclear tests—the destruction of people, genetic consequences, and all these things.

And I was, as it happened, at that moment very far from the basic problems of all of the people and of the whole country. I found myself in an extraordinary position of material privilege and isolated from the people.

*But after that?*

After that my life began to change in purely personal terms, psychologically. And the process of development simply went further . . .

Now, what is socialism? I began by thinking that I understood it and that it was good. Then gradually I ceased to understand a great deal—I didn't even understand its economic [basis]; I couldn't make out whether there was anything to it but mere words and propaganda for internal and international consumption. Actually, what hits you in the eye is the state's extreme concentration—economic, political, and ideological—that is, its extreme monopolization of these fields. One may say, exactly as Lenin did at the beginning of our revolution, that it is simple state capitalism, that the state has simply assumed a monopoly role over all the economy. But in that case this socialism contains nothing new. It is only an extreme form of that capitalist path of development found in the United States and other Western countries but in an extremely monopolized form. Thus, we should not be surprised that we have the same kinds of problems—that is, crime and personal alienation—that are to be found in the capitalist world. But our society represents an extreme case with maximum restraint, maximum ideological restrictions, and so forth. . . . Moreover, and very characteristically, we are also the most pretentious—that is, although we are not the best society we pretend that we are much more . . .

*What concrete shortcomings do you see in today's Soviet society?*

In the lack of freedom, to be certain. In lack of freedom, in the bureaucratization of government, in its extremely irrational and also terribly egoistic—that is, class-egoistic—tendency that actually aims only at preserving the system, maintaining a good appearance to conceal a very unpleasant internal state of affairs. A society on the decline. But I've already written about that. And it must be very widely known to attentive observers that for us all social things are more for show than for reality. This relates to education, to its organization, and to medical services. Very often people from the West say: "Well, you have many faults but at least you have free medical service." But actually it is no more free than in many Western countries and often it is even less free, so to speak, because its general quality is so low.

*Do you think that Soviet society today is a class society?*

Well, that is again a theoretical question—that is a question requiring a theoretical evaluation. But in any case it is a society of great internal inequality . . . Can we say from this that it has a class structure? It is in a certain sense a distinctive society. It is hard to say whether it should be called a class society. In a sense this is a matter of definition. It's something like our past arguments as to what kind of society could be called fascist. It is also a question of definition, a question of terminology.

*But what about the inequality?*

Inequality. Inequality arises on a very large number of levels. There is inequality between village people and city people; the collective farmers do not have passports, which means that in practical terms they are bound to their place of residence on the collective farm. And only if they can get permission (true, it is ordinarily given) may they leave the collective farm. There is inequality among regions: Moscow and the larger cities are favored in the distribution of products, living comforts, cultural services, and so on. And the [internal] passport system strengthens these territorial inequities. Most unfairly treated is . . .

*Andrei Dmitrivich, you have yourself said that you are privileged . . .*

Yes, I have been privileged, of course, and still am today through inertia. I was privileged in the past, actually hyper-privileged, because I was a worker at the very pinnacle of the arms industry. I had by Soviet standards a colossal salary and bonuses.

*And, in your opinion, what privileges do Party figures have in the Soviet Union?*

Well, they have great extrafinancial privileges. There are the following: a system of sanitariums, medical services . . . great privileges. Real privileges arise, you might say, from personal connections, personal factors of various kinds. Privileges in work, in one's career. All positions of any importance, like those of factory director, chief engineer, and so on are held only by Party members. Exceptions are very rare. And the shop chief must be a Party member. So everything depends on Party membership, on your situation in the Party structure or your official . . . These things have enormous influence on your career. And, in addition, there is the traditional attitude toward Party cadres that is expressed in what is called *nomenklatura*. This means that even if a person fails in some kind of work, as long as he is a leading Party worker he will be trans-

ferred to some other job not very different in material advantages from the one he gives up.

The whole manner of getting a job and advancement
is very strongly connected with interrelationships within
the system. Each important administrator has attached to
him personally certain people who move with him from
place to place as he is transferred. There is something ir-
resistible about this and it seems to be a kind of law of our
state structure.

But if we talk about material advantages, then the
basic advantage consists in the rise of a kind of isolated but
more or less well-defined group that has a special relationship to the government. The advantages are determined by
Party membership but there are also within the Party very
large distinctions. It seems as though something like Orwell's concept of an inner party already exists with us in a
certain sense.

And if we talk about people in this inner Party, then
they have great material advantages. There exists a system
of supplemental pay in [special] envelopes. This system
sometimes disappears and then again reappears. I don't
know what the situation is at the given moment, but it
looks as though the custom has been revived in some
places. Then there is the supplemental system of so-called
closed shops, where not only is the quality of the products
better and the assortment wider but also the price differs
from the general price structure so that with the same ruble
these people can buy a different product at a different
price and that means the arithmetical figure of their wage
is not really very significant.*

_____

* After reading the text of the interview Sakharov offered the following
clarification: "In that part of the interview devoted to the privileged
position of the members of the Party there may be created the false im-

*We have talked a lot about shortcomings. Now, of course, we must take up the question of what can be done to correct all this.*

What can be done and what should be strived for are different questions. It seems to me that almost nothing can be done ...

*Why not?*

Because the system has a very strong internal stability. The less free a system is the greater ordinarily its ability to maintain itself.

*And outside forces can do nothing?*

We have a very poor understanding of what the foreign world is doing. Possibly the foreign world will soon accept our rules of the game. That would be very bad. But there is, of course, another side to the matter. We are now breaking out of our fifty-year isolation and possibly with time this may even exert a beneficial influence. But how this will all come out—it is very difficult to predict. And if we speak of the West, then it is difficult each time to tell whether they want to help us or whether, on the contrary, there is some kind of capitulation, a game involving the internal interests of the people of the West in which we merely play the role of small change.

*Well, those are foreign forces—what about inside the Soviet Union?*

Within the Soviet Union certainly some kind of pro-

pression that Party members and non-Party members in the same job receive different salaries. That is not so and I want to correct this inexactitude. However, what is said regarding the influence of Party membership on a career, the Party hierarchy, etc. remains in force."

cess is going on, but so far it is so imperceptible and hidden that it's not possible to forecast anything positive, any general change, and as for positive things . . . well, it's almost impossible. We understand that such a large state as ours can never be homogeneous but in the absence of information and the absence of contacts between separate groups of people it is almost impossible to understand what is going on. But we know that there are very strong nationalistic tendencies on the periphery of our state. Whether they are positive or not is very hard to determine in individual cases. In some cases—for example, in the Ukraine—they have become very strongly interwoven with democratic forces. In the Baltic states it is the same— religious and nationalist forces have become interwoven very naturally and easily with the democratic. But in other places it may not be the same. We don't know in detail.

*So you are very skeptical in spite of the fact that you yourself . . .*

I am skeptical about socialism in general. I don't see that socialism offers some kind of new theoretical plan, so to speak, for the better organization of society. Therefore it seems to me that while in our diverse system of life we may find some positive variants, on the whole our state has displayed more destructive features than positive ones. The positive features may be said to be the result of more general human factors—and they are not few—but they are human factors, which could have arisen in another environment, while in our society there have arisen such fierce political struggles, such destruction, such bitterness that now we are reaping the sad fruits of all this in a kind of tiredness, apathy, cynicism, a kind of . . . which we find it most difficult to recover, or indeed, to recover in general. What direction of development our society will take is extremely difficult to predict from within. Perhaps it can be done better from the outside, but for this, one requires the maximum in objectivity.

*But, Andrei Dmitrivich, you are doubtful that any-thing in general can be done to improve the system of the Soviet Union, yet you yourself go ahead acting, writing declarations, protests—why?*

Well, there is a need to create ideals even when you can't see any route by which to achieve them, because if there are no ideals then there can be no hope and then one would be completely in the dark, in a hopeless blind alley.

Moreover, we can't know whether there is some kind of possibility of cooperation between our country and the outside world. If no signals about our unhappy situation are sent out, then there cannot be . . . then even the pos-sibility, which might exist, could not be utilized, because we wouldn't know what it was that needed to be changed or how to change it.

Then there is the other consideration—that the history of our country should be some kind of warning. It should hold back the West and the developing countries from committing mistakes on such a scale as we have done dur-ing our historical development. Therefore, if a man does not keep silent it does not mean that he hopes necessarily to achieve something. These are not the same question. He may hope for nothing but nonetheless speak because he cannot, simply cannot remain silent.

In almost every concrete case of repression we really

have no hope and almost always there is a tragic absence of positive results.

*But what is it that you are aiming at?*
In what sense? In a social sense?

*Yes.*
Well, in the sense of an ideal I attempted in my memorandum [to General Secretary Brezhnev] and especially in the postscript to it to express a certain ideal, but in the memorandum there is much I should myself correct, because it was written a long time ago, in 1971, and it was published a year and a half later without changes. For instance, I wrote then about the Chinese problem in a tone I would not use today, because at that time I simply did not understand our relations with China and if you do not understand then it is better not to write. For example, I would not now blame China for aggression. But I didn't say even that very clearly and perhaps there was an element of overemphasis on the Chinese threats. As for China itself, it simply represents a much earlier stage of development in our society and it is directed more toward revolutionary self-assertion both internally and in the outer world than, for example, with achieving prosperity for her people and expanding her territory. Probably they don't see this as a problem. China is very similar to Russia in the 1920's and the beginning of the 1930's.

*But if you think that socialism in the Soviet Union has not shown its superiority, does that mean you think that in order to remedy the situation you must therefore reconstruct the whole state or can something be done within the system in order to improve it and eliminate its greatest defects?*

That is too difficult a question for me, because to re-organize the state—that is unthinkable; there always must be some kind of continuity and some kind of gradualness, otherwise there would again be the terrible destruction through which we have passed several times and a total collapse. Thus, I, of course, am inclined to gradualness. I am a liberal or a "gradualist," if you please.

*Well, what is to be done first?*

What must be done? I think that our present system can do nothing or at least very little by its own internal resources. What must be done? We must liquidate the ideological monism of our society.

*Excuse me—what?*

The ideological structure that is anti-democratic in its very essence—it has been very tragic for the state. Isolation from the outside world. For example, the absence of the right to leave and to return produces a very pernicious effect on the internal life of the country. It is in the first instance a great tragedy for all those who wish to leave for personal or national reasons. But it is also a tragedy for those who remain in the country, because a country from which it is not possible to leave freely, to which it is not possible to return freely is a country that is defective, a closed volume where all processes develop differently from those of an open system.

*You know that the right of free exit . . .*

. . . is one of the very important conditions for return, for free return.

*And what else?*

It is one of the conditions the country needs for developing along healthier lines. But there are things of an economic nature that are more important. Our very extreme state socialism has led to the closing down of private initiative in areas in which it would be most effective, just as private initiative has been eliminated in large-scale industry and in transport, in which perhaps the state system of administration is more sensible. Moreover, the simple personal initiative of citizens and their personal freedom have been very restricted. This is reflected negatively in the people's way of living and simply makes life much more boring and dreary than need be. I am talking about personal initiative in the field of consumer goods, education, and medicine. All of this no doubt would have a very positive significance in weakening the extreme monopolistic structure of the state. There are aspects relative to the monopoly of administration—that is, the Party monopoly of administration—which with us have reached unheard-of levels . . . it must even be evident at the leadership level that these aspects are intolerable. It already has begun to influence the effectiveness of administration.

So—what is needed? We need first of all greater openness in the work of the administrative apparatus. Quite possibly the single-party system is excessively and unnecessarily rigid. Even under the conditions of a socialist economic system the one-party system is not necessary. Actually, on some levels of the peoples democracies, the one-party system is not needed. And in some of the peoples democracies some elements, so to speak, of a multiparty system exist although in a semicaricatured style.

We need elections to state organs with a certain

number of candidates. In general, a series of measures that taken individually would have little effect but that in combination might shake that monolith we have created, which is so fossilized and so oppressive on the life of the whole country.

The press must change its character. Now it is so standardized that it has lost any significant informational value. And when it does reflect facts, they are expressed in such a way that they are understandable only to the initiated and reflect a distorted picture of real life in the country. As for intellectual life, it simply does not exist so that there is nothing there that can be distorted since there is no variety in intellectual life.

One thing must be emphasized, and that is the role of the intelligentsia in society. It is quite illegally suppressed. It is materially badly off. It is not distinguished from physical work and is poorly provided for. And in absolute terms its living standard is very low in comparison with Western countries that have reached a comparable stage of development. The oppressed situation of the intelligentsia and its economic oppression as well mean ideological oppression, which is reflected in a certain anti-intellectual atmosphere in the country, in which the intellectual professions, the professions of teachers, of doctors, do not receive the respect they should have. And the anti-intellectualism is reflected in the fact that the intelligentsia itself has begun to retreat into narrow professionalism, into a kind of dual intellectual life at work and at home, into narrow circles of their own friends, where people begin to think in different ways, and this dichotomy leads to hypocrisy and a further fall in the morals and creativity of people. The results are particularly sharp in the human-

istic as distinguished from the technical intelligentsia.
They feel that they have gotten into a kind of blind alley.
As a result, the literature that appears is terribly gray or
conventional and generally boring. Literature, art, the
cinema begin ...

*Permit me one last question. You personally have
never feared for your health and freedom in these years in
which you have been so active?*

Not very much. I have not feared for myself, but that
is, you might say, part of my character and partly because
I began from a very high social position, where such fears
were perfectly unjustified and irrelevant. But now I have
grounds for fearing such forms of pressure, which are
not directed against me personally but against members
of my family, members of the family of my wife. That is
the most painful thing, because it is very real and is coming
closer to us. Such things as happened to [Veniamin] Levich
[corresponding member of the Academy of Sciences] when
his son was picked up; this shows how they go about these
things.

*July 3, 1973*

# INTERVIEW WITH MIKHAIL P. MALYAROV, FIRST DEPUTY SOVIET PROSECUTOR

On August 15, I received a telephone call from the Deputy Prosecutor General and was asked to come to see him. He did not say what it was about, asserting simply that it would be a man-to-man talk. I arrived at the Prosecutor's office on August 16 at noon and was met at the gate by an employee who took me into the building; another then accompanied me to an office where I was received by M. P. Malyarov, the Deputy Prosecutor General, and another man who introduced himself only as Malyarov's assistant. He took notes and participated in the conversation.

Below I have reproduced the seventy-minute conversation from memory, and the reconstruction may therefore contain some paraphrases, minor unintentional abridgments, and inversions in sequence.

□

MALYAROV: This conversation is intended to be in the nature of a warning and not all my statements will be supported by detailed proof, but you can believe me that we have such proof. Please listen to me attentively and try not to interrupt.

SAKHAROV: I am listening.

MALYAROV: When you began a few years ago to engage in what you call public activity, we could not possibly ignore it and we paid close attention. We assumed that you would express your opinions as a Soviet citizen about certain shortcomings and errors, as you see them, without attacking the Soviet social and political system as such. To be sure, even then your statements were being published in the anti-Soviet press abroad and they caused noticeable harm to our country. Lately your activity and statements have assumed an even more harmful and openly anti-Soviet character and cannot be overlooked by the Prosecutor's office, which is charged with enforcing the law and protecting the interests of society. You are seeing foreigners and giving them material for anti-Soviet publications. That applies in particular to your interview with the Swedish radio. In that interview you denounced the socialist system in our country, calling it a system of maximum nonfreedom, a system that is undemocratic, closed, deprived of economic initiative, and falling to pieces.

SAKHAROV: I did not say "falling to pieces."

MALYAROV: You keep meeting with reactionary newsmen, like the Swedish radio correspondent Stenholm, and give them interviews that are then used for subversive propaganda and are printed by Possev, the publishing arm of the NTS [a Russian émigré organization with head-quarters in Frankfurt, West Germany]. You must be aware that the NTS program calls for the overthrow of the Soviet regime. Possev publishes more of your writings than any-one else, and in your interview you adopted in effect the same anti-Soviet subversive position.

SAKHAROV: I am not familiar with the NTS program. If it does indeed include such a plank, it would be funda-mentally opposed to my views, as stated, for example, in the interview with the Swedish Radio. There I spoke about the desirability of gradual change, about democratization within the framework of the present system. Of course, I am also referring to what I consider serious faults in the system and do not conceal my pessimism (with regard to possible changes in the near future). As for those publica-tions, I never handed over any material for the NTS or for Possev, and my writings have appeared in many foreign mass media besides Possev. For example, in *Der Spiegel* [West German news magazine], which the Soviet press has regarded as rather progressive so far.

MALYAROV'S ASSISTANT: But you never protested pub-lication in Possev. We found that most of your writings appeared in Possev, *Grani* [another publication of Possev], and the White Guards newspaper *Russkaya Mysl* [of Paris].

SAKHAROV: I would be very glad to have my writings published in the Soviet press. For example, if, in addition to [Yuri] Kornilov's critical article, *Literaturnaya Gazeta* [Soviet Weekly] had also published my interview [with the Swedish Radio]. In that case Kornilov would not have been able to distort the interview. But that is obviously out of the question. I consider openness of publication of great importance. I consider the content of publications far more important than the place of publication.

MALYAROV'S ASSISTANT: Even if they appear in anti-Soviet publications for anti-Soviet purposes, as in Possev?

SAKHAROV: I consider Possev's publishing activities highly useful. I am grateful to that publisher. I reserve the right not to identify Possev with the NTS and not to approve of the NTS program, with which I am not even familiar, or to condemn those aspects of NTS activities that may be viewed as provocative (like sending Sokolov as a witness to the Galanskov–Ginzburg trial, which did have such consequences). [The reference is to Nicolas Brocks Sokolov, an NTS courier, who was arrested on arriving in the Soviet Union and testified for the prosecution in the 1968 trial of two dissidents.]

MALYAROV'S ASSISTANT: We are not talking about that now, that was a long time ago.

SAKHAROV: To go back, you called Stenholm [of the Swedish Radio] a reactionary journalist. That is unfair. He is a Social Democrat; he is far more of a socialist or Communist than I am, for example.

MALYAROV'S ASSISTANT: The Social Democrats were the ones who murdered Rosa Luxemburg [German Communist, in 1919]. As for that "Communist" of yours, he evidently inserted into your interview that our system was "falling to pieces," if indeed you did not say it.

SAKHAROV: I am convinced that Stenholm quoted me correctly.

MALYAROV: Let me go on. Please listen closely. By nature of your previous work, you had access to state secrets of particular importance. You signed a commitment not to divulge state secrets and not to meet with foreigners. But you do meet with foreigners and you are giving them information that may be of interest to foreign intelligence agencies. I am asking you to consider this a serious warning and to draw your conclusions.

SAKHAROV: I insist that I have never divulged any military or military-technical secrets that I may have known by nature of my work from 1948 to 1968. And I never intend to do so. I also want to call your attention to the fact that I have been out of secret work for the last five years.

MALYAROV: But you still have your head on your shoulders, and your pledge not to meet with foreigners is still in effect. You are beginning to be used not only by anti-Soviet forces hostile to our country, but also by foreign intelligence.

SAKHAROV: As for meetings with foreigners, I know many people who used to be in my position and who now meet freely with foreign scholars and ordinary citizens. I do meet with some foreign journalists, but those meetings have no bearing whatever on any state, military, or military-technical secrets.

MALYAROV'S ASSISTANT: Those meetings are of benefit to our enemies.

MALYAROV: We have now warned you. It is up to you to draw your conclusions.

SAKHAROV: I repeat. I would prefer to be published in the Soviet press and to deal with Soviet institutions. But I see nothing illegal in meeting with foreign journalists.

MALYAROV'S ASSISTANT: But you are still a Soviet citizen. Your qualification shows your real attitude toward our system.

SAKHAROV: Soviet institutions ignore my letters and other forms of communication. If we just take the Prosecutor's office, I remember that in May 1970 (I think it was May 17), several persons, including myself, addressed a complaint to Comrade [Roman A.] Rudenko, the Prosecutor General, in the case of [Maj. Gen. Pyotr G.] Grigorenko [a dissident committed to a psychiatric hospital in 1969]. There were many gross violations of the law in that case. There has been no reply to that complaint to this day. Many times I did not even receive confirmation of the delivery of my letters. The late Academician Petrovsky, who was a member of the Presidium of the Supreme Soviet of the USSR [Ivan G. Petrovsky, rector of Moscow University, died in 1973], promised to look into the case of the psychiatrist Semyon Gluzman, sentenced in Kiev in 1972 in a trial fraught with violations of the law. That was the only time anyone promised to look into a case for me. But Petrovsky is now dead. And how about the Amalrik case? [Andrei A. Amalrik, dissident author.] He was unjustly sentenced to three years, he lost his health, suffered from meningitis, and now he has been sentenced in a labor-camp court to another three years. It is an absolute disgrace. He was in fact sentenced once again for his convictions, which he has refused to recant and does not force on anyone. And a labor-camp court! What kind of public proceeding, what kind of justice is that?

MALYAROV: That Amalrik is a half-educated student. He contributed nothing to the state. He was a parasite. And Böll [Heinrich Böll, West German author] writes about him as if he were an outstanding historian. Is that the kind of information Böll has?

SAKHAROV: Böll and many others demonstrate a great deal of interest in Amalrik's fate. A labor-camp court is in fact a closed court.

MALYAROV: I suppose you would have brought him to Moscow for trial?

SAKHAROV: In view of the wide public interest, that would have made sense. If I had known that I could have attended Amalrik's trial, I would have done so.

MALYAROV: Amalrik caused a great deal of harm to our society. In one of his books he tried to show that Soviet society would not survive until 1984, and in so doing he called for violent action. Any society has the right to defend itself. Amalrik violated the law, and he must take the punishment. In camp he again violated the law. You know the law, I don't have to tell you what it is. Abroad they wrote that Amalrik was deprived of a lawyer. That is a lie. Shveisky [Vladimir Shveisky, Amalrik's lawyer] attended the trial, and you know that.

MALYAROV'S ASSISTANT: In contrast to that dropout, you did make contributions to society.

MALYAROV: Who gave you the right to doubt our system of justice? You did not attend the trial. You base yourself on rumors, and they are often wrong.

SAKHAROV: When proceedings are not public, when political trials are consistently held under conditions allowing for violations, there are grounds for doubting the fairness of the court. I consider it undemocratic to prosecute under Articles 190–1 [on circulating false information defaming the Soviet state] and 70 [on anti-Soviet agitation and propaganda]. All the cases with which I am familiar confirm this. Take the recent case of Leonid Plyushch [a Kiev mathematician]. In that case, the court accepted the most grievous of three contradictory psychiatric findings without checking any of them. Although the court reduced the sentence, it was restored upon protest by the prosecution. Plyushch is being kept in a special [psychiatric] hospital, and his wife has not seen him for more than a year and a half.

MALYAROV: You keep dealing in legal questions, but you don't seem to know them very well. The court has the power to determine the form of compulsory treatment regardless of the findings of an expert commission.

SAKHAROV: I am unfortunately all too familiar with that. And, therefore, even when the expert commission recommends an ordinary hospital, there are grounds for fearing the worst. You say I always rely on rumor. That is not so. I try to get reliable information. But it is becoming increasingly difficult in this country to know what is going on. There is no publication with complete and precise information about violations [of due process].

MALYAROV'S ASSISTANT: You mean the *Chronicle* [the *Chronicle of Current Events,* an underground publication that has not appeared since October 1972]?

SAKHAROV: Of course.

MALYAROV'S ASSISTANT: You will soon be hearing about the *Chronicle*. You know what I mean. But now we are talk-about more important matters.

MALYAROV: You don't seem to like the fact that our [Criminal] Code contains Article 190-1 and 70. But there they are. The state has the right to defend itself. You must know what you are doing. I am not going to try to convince you. I know that would be useless. But you must understand what is involved here. And who is supporting you, anyway, who needs you? Yakir, whom you know well, was written about constantly in the anti-Soviet press abroad as long as he provided it with propaganda. As soon as he changed his views, he was forgotten. [Pyotr Yakir was arrested in June 1972 and is now being tried.]

SAKHAROV: To say that I know him well is not correct. I hardly know him. But I do know that there is great interest in his case. Everyone is wondering when the trial will begin. Do you know?

MALYAROV'S ASSISTANT: No. When the trial starts, you will probably know about it yourself.

MALYAROV: Your friend Chalidze [Valery Chalidze, now living in the United States] was quite famous in the West as long as he came out with anti-Soviet statements, and when he stopped he was also soon forgotten. Anti-Soviet circles need people like [Julius] Telesin, [Vladimir] Telnikov [dissidents living in Great Britain], and Volpin [Alexander Volpin, now living in the United States], who keep slandering their former homeland.

SAKHAROV: I don't think that Chalidze ever engaged in anti-Soviet activity. The same goes for the others. You mentioned Volpin. As far as I know, he is busy with mathematics in Boston.

MALYAROV: That may be, but we also have reliable information about his anti-Soviet activity.

SAKHAROV: You say that no one is supporting me. Last year I took part in two collective appeals, for amnesty and for abolition of the death penalty. Each of these appeals was signed by more than fifty persons.

MALYAROV: Only asking that the matter be considered?

SAKHAROV: Yes. And we were quite distressed when the law on amnesty turned out to be a very limited one, and the death penalty was not abolished.

MALYAROV: You did not seriously expect a change in the law just because you wanted it. This is not the time to abolish the death penalty. Murderers and rapists who commit serious crimes go unpunished. [The death penalty also applies to serious crimes against the state, such as treason and espionage and economic crimes.]

SAKHAROV: I am talking about abolishing the very institution of the death penalty. Many thoughtful people are of the view that this institution has no place in a humane society and that it is immoral. We have serious crime despite the existence of the death penalty. The death penalty does not help make society more humane. I heard that abolition of the death penalty has been under discussion in Soviet legal circles.

MALYAROV: No. One jurist raised the question, but he found no support. The time is not ripe.

SAKHAROV: The issue is now being debated throughout the world. Many countries have abolished the death penalty. Why should we be different?

MALYAROV: They abolished it in the United States, but now they are forced to restore it. You've been reading about the crimes that have occurred there. Nothing like that happens here. You seem to like the American way of life even though they permit the unrestricted sale of guns, they murder their Presidents, and now they've got this demagogic fraud of the Watergate case. Sweden, too, is proud of her freedom, and they have pornographic pictures on every street. I saw them myself. Don't tell me you are for pornography, for that kind of freedom?

SAKHAROV: I am not familiar with either the American or the Swedish way of life. They probably have their own problems and I would not idealize them. But you mentioned the Watergate case. To me, it is a good illustration of American democracy.

MALYAROV: It is calculated to be just a show. All Nixon has to do is show a little firmness, and the whole thing will come to nothing. That's their democracy for you, nothing but a fraud. I think we should end this conversation. There was one more thing. You seem to have a high opinion of Belinkov [Arkady V. Belinkov, a Soviet writer who defected to the West in 1968 and died two years later]. You know that name, don't you?

SAKHAROV: I consider Belinkov an outstanding writer on public affairs. I particularly appreciated his letter to the

Pen Club in 1968 [protesting curbs on intellectual freedom in the Soviet Union].

MALYAROV: Are you aware that Belinkov was once arrested and imprisoned for having distributed leaflets calling for the killing of Communists?

SAKHAROV: I don't know anything about that. That probably happened a long time ago under Stalin. How can you take that seriously? At that time anyone could be arrested as a terrorist.

MALYAROV: No, Belinkov was imprisoned twice, the second time not so long ago. And how about your Daniel [Yuli M. Daniel, dissident writer, who served five years at hard labor, from 1966 to 1970]? Didn't he call openly for the murder of leaders of the Party and government in his story "Day of Open Murders"? And Amalrik, is he any better? You should think about it.

SAKHAROV: "Day of Open Murders" is a work of fiction, an allegory, directed in spirit against the terror of the Stalin years, which was still very fresh at that time, in 1956. Daniel made that quite clear in his trial. As for [Amalrik's] "Will the USSR Survive until 1984?"—that, too, is an allegory. You know that the date stems from Orwell's story.

MALYAROV: We had better stop. I just want you to give serious thought to my warning. Any state has the right to defend itself. There are appropriate articles in the Criminal Code, and no one will be permitted to violate them.

SAKHAROV: I have been listening closely and I will certainly bear in mind every word you said. But I cannot agree that I have been violating the law. In particular, I cannot agree with your statement that my meetings with foreign correspondents are illegal or that they endanger state secrets. Goodbye.

MALYAROV: Goodbye.

*August 16, 1973*

# INTERVIEW WITH FOREIGN CORRESPONDENTS

SAKHAROV: All those present are familiar with the record of my conversation with M. P. Malyarov, the First Deputy Prosecutor General (on August 16). Please consider that record as an introduction to our conversation today.

I would like to make some additional comments:

First, about the practice of issuing "warnings": various forms of "warnings" have been employed recently with dissidents by the State Security Committee (KGB) and associated agencies. In some cases such warnings have preceded arrest, in other cases they have been followed by permission to emigrate. The particular form of warning that I encountered August 16 is undoubtedly more serious than the one given me last March at the KGB, when my wife and I offered to become surety in the case of Yury Shikhanovich [a Moscow University mathematician arrested September

28, 1972, and held incommunicado since then. The Sa-
kharovs' offer of being guarantors was refused].

On the other hand, there are even more serious forms
of warnings. It was learned recently that several persons
had been "warned" that their fates would depend on testimony they gave at forthcoming trials. If their behavior as
witnesses was not satisfactory, it was said, then they would
not "leave the courtroom."

No less ominous, and reviving the institution of hostages, were widely publicized "warnings" that for the appearance of every new issue of the *Chronicle of Current
Events* (the underground news bulletin), appropriate persons would be arrested and those already under arrest
would be sentenced to long terms.

The articles about me that have appeared in the Soviet
press are also likely to be intended as "warnings," from the
standpoint of the KGB. When I discussed the Shikhanovich
case with the KGB, I was told that he had not drawn the
proper conclusions from his "warnings," which in this case
apparently referred to searches of his home.

In general, the system of "warnings" seems designed
to remind people of the existence of a force that will not
tolerate any deviation from a desired line on the presumed
grounds that "a state has the right to self-defense." If this
interpretation of the "warnings" is correct, they are symp-
tomatic of the kind of thinking found in police agencies,
and have nothing in common with democracy or the right
to one's convictions, or the law, or humanity.

Second, regarding the NTS [a Russian émigré organization based in Frankfurt, West Germany] and Possev [its
publishing house]. Accusations that writings or appeals are
being used in anti-Soviet publications of Possev for "anti-

Soviet subversive purposes" have become the principal
bogy used by the KGB and its like; they have become the
principal accusation and the most important means of in-
timidation and of exerting pressure on public opinion. Even
the most casual possession of a Possev publication is regarded as a crime. It is very important, therefore, that this
issue be clarified. As for me, in my conversation in the
Prosecutor's office, I welcomed the publishing and enlight-
enment activities of Possev, without regard to the program
of the NTS (which aims at the overthrow of the Soviet
regime) or to the actions and statements of particular representatives of that organization, with which I do not necessarily have to sympathize.

Third, as for the Prosecutor's contention that my meetings with foreigners violate previous pledges. In 1950, when
I went to work in a classified institution, I did indeed sign
an undertaking that made any meetings with foreigners
punishable "by administrative procedures." The maximum
administrative penalty is dismissal from work. I was dismissed from the job in 1968, after publication of my essay
*Progress, Coexistence, and Intellectual Freedom,* long before I ever met any foreigner. I can only repeat here what
I told Malyarov, namely that my meetings with foreign
journalists have no bearing whatever on any violation of
state secrets, which I would never and under no circumstances consider permissible.

*Do you regard the talk at the Prosecutor's office and
the* Tass *attack as a general warning or as directed specifically at your interview with the Swedish radio?*
The interview was evidently the last drop that filled
the cup to overflowing. Someone must have authorized the

summons to the Prosecutor's office. It could have been authorized at the highest level. But it could also have been sanctioned at an intermediate level so that no one could be reproached for not having warned me. However, I consider this less likely than the first alternative.

*Do you think the authorities distinguish between your work within the Committee for Human Rights and your personal criticism of the Soviet system?*

Neither one is evidently acceptable to them, but in different degrees.

*Could you develop that thought further?*

The Committee, of which I am only a member, is, of course, a totally loyal association. In the interview with the Swedish radio, I expressed my personal opinions. I do not impose these opinions on anyone, but they were evidently found unacceptable in substance.

*Do you get the impression that the authorities want you to leave the country? Was it that kind of a warning?*

This was never openly suggested to me, nor was it in this latest conversation. In fact, I was told that I am still a Soviet citizen. I interpret this to mean that I should stop doing what I am doing in this country, not that I am invited to leave the country.

*Were you threatened in some other way? Directly or indirectly?*

No. I tried to write down a full account of the conversation. Nothing else was said. They evidently thought I understood the point well enough.

*Have you personally ever considered leaving the Soviet Union?*

I have always replied to that question that I am not ripe for such a decision.

*What do you think will be the next step?*

I have already had the occasion to state that I fear most those forms of pressure that are not directed against me personally but could become indirectly unbearable and intolerable.

*Do you mean your family?*

I mean my family or other persons dear to me. I can really not predict what may happen. Of course, steps may also be taken against me personally but I like to believe that the loyal character of my activities will ultimately be understood.

*Loyal to what?*

Loyal in the literal meaning of the word, namely lawful.

*I have a more general question. People often wonder what your means of support is and what work you are doing.*

First of all, I get a salary from the Lebedev Institute of Physics, where I hold the post of Senior Research Associate, the lowest position that can be given a member of the Academy of Sciences. In addition I receive my honorarium as a member of the Academy.

*What amounts are involved?*

As a member of the Academy four hundred rubles a

month, and in the Institute job three hundred and fifty rubles. I have already stated that I contributed all my savings in 1969 to a government fund for the building of a new cancer research center.

*How much was that?*
A very large sum. A hundred and thirty-nine thousand rubles.

*What made you contribute such a large sum?*
In hindsight, I consider it completely senseless; I do not think I was right to do it so I won't give the reasons.

*You say that you are on the staff of the Physics Institute. Does that mean that you are in fact working there?*
That is a difficult question for me to answer. In general, productivity in theoretical physics tends to decline at my age. That is the general rule. Furthermore, my work in theoretical physics was interrupted for a long time while I was employed in applied fields. And finally, inner unrest also has not made it any easier. In short, I have not been productive in recent years. I am still hopeful that this is a temporary situation and that I will still accomplish something but I can't pretend to hope too much.

*Do you actually go to the Institute?*
I do, although a theoretical physicist is actually supposed to work at home, with journals, and with a piece of paper and a pen.

*What relations do you have with your former colleagues?*

They have become very weak. I see them seldom, and very few of them.

*Are your colleagues trying to put pressure on you to induce you to change your position?*
No, no one is trying to do that. With only rare exceptions.

*Do you interpret their silence as approval of your stand?*
Rather as reluctance to get involved in delicate matters. Although both may be true.

*How widespread, in your view, is a desire for democratization among the intelligentsia?*
It is very difficult for me to speak for the intelligentsia. It would require a major sociological research effort.

*How many members of your family have already been under some form of pressure?*
Those members of my family on my wife's side. Her daughter [by a previous marriage], Tatyana Ivanovna Semyonova, born in February 1950, has been barred from her last year in the University. Her brother, Aleksei, born in 1956, has been denied admission to the University, which is also a form of pressure. He was told that he was "marked." In a more indirect form, my stepdaughter's husgand, Yefrem V. Yankelevich, twenty-three, was dismissed from his job after he applied to go to the Massachusetts Institute of Technology for study. He graduated from the Institute of Communications and now has a temporary job with a geophysical expedition. All three had been invited by Dr. Jerome B. Wiesner, the president of MIT, with the

promise of scholarships. There has been no answer to the applications, which were handed in last April 6. The applications have not even been acknowledged. When I inquired, I was told, "This is not a trip to Penza Province [in central Russia]," and they had to take their time about it.

*Is it not unusual for Soviet citizens to apply to go abroad individually for study?*
Very unusual. But anywhere else in the world, it is highly usual. Here everything is unusual. Nevertheless, the Soviet Union has an agreement with the United States covering student exchanges, so these applications should not really be considered all that unusual.

*Didn't you also have an invitation to go to the United States?*
Yes, I did get an invitation from Princeton for one academic year. I was very interested and would be glad to go, but I have not taken any steps so far. The question is a very complicated one.

*Do you see any pattern in the tactics now being used toward dissidents? Some are allowed to leave the country. Others are being put on trial. Still others are being committed to mental institutions. How do you explain the various approaches being used?*
I believe many considerations enter into each particular case. The combination of all three techniques seems to offer the greatest flexibility.

*Even among those who are allowed to leave the country and whose Soviet citizenship is then canceled, the approach also seems to differ. Valery Chalidze was deprived of his citizenship promptly upon his arrival in the United States. Zhores Medvedev had to wait much longer.*

Yes, evidently here, too, no standard method is being followed.

*What is your general evaluation of the present state of the democratic movement in the Soviet Union?*

I have always found it difficult to consider it a movement as such. I have viewed it essentially as an expression of concern for the fate of particular persons who have become the victims of injustice. I have considered it mainly as an effort to protest against unfair trials, unjustified commitments to mental institutions, to help the families of the persons concerned. It is certainly not a movement of any kind. It is normal human activity that cannot be regarded as political. There is, of course, also another aspect. There are people who want to assert the right to freedom of conviction for themselves and for others. These convictions may also vary widely, so that here again it would be difficult to speak of a movement as such. So that if you view the situation from the bottom up, there is no movement that may be regarded as pursuing a particular political goal, such as a struggle for power. Even if you were to view the situation from the top, it seems to me that it would be difficult to discern a movement. So that the authorities really have no grounds for concern, especially not for any repressions. If there are any grounds for concern, these must be within their minds.

*But if you compare the present situation to the past, say, two years ago, there was more of the type of activity you have described.*

If we take those about whose fate we have been concerned I must admit that their ranks have been thinned simply as a result of intensified repression. It represents an injustice, a great personal tragedy for a large number of people. It has had a negative impact on the psychological climate within the country. It has also had a negative impact on the international situation. On the whole, I do not consider the intensification of repressions to have been a sensible decision by the authorities. Just as I did not see any sense in the events whose fifth anniversary we are marking today. I am referring to the news learned on August 21, 1968, by Soviet citizens that a group of political figures had appealed for help to protect the gains of socialism in Czechoslovakia. Exactly five years ago Czechoslovakia was invaded. Now we've all forgotten about it.

*If you do not consider the present policy [toward dissidents] to be sensible, why do you think it is being pursued?*

I believe that the people at the top of our society have developed a particular way of thinking. They probably see no other way of reacting to the present situation.

*May I ask you about your essay* Progress, Coexistence, and Intellectual Freedom, *which was published five years ago? If you think back to the analysis of world prospects you then presented, how has the situation in fact evolved, in your view?*

I discussed the possible evolution of events in terms of certain time spans, and these should be viewed as allegorical. But my basic premise still holds true, namely that the world faces two alternatives—either gradual convergence with democratization within the Soviet Union, or increasing confrontation with a growing danger of thermonuclear war. But reality has turned out to be trickier, in the sense that we now face a very specific issue: Will rapprochement be associated with democratization of Soviet society or not? This new alternative, which at first sight may seem a half-way measure, better than nothing, in fact conceals within itself a great internal danger.

*What alternative are you now referring to?*

I mean rapprochement without democratization, rapprochement in which the West in effect accepts the Soviet Union rules of the game. Such a rapprochement would be dangerous in the sense that it would not really solve any of the world's problems and would mean simply capitulating in the face of real or exaggerated Soviet power. It would mean an attempt to trade with the Soviet Union, buying its gas and oil, while ignoring all other aspects. I think such a development would be dangerous because it would have serious repercussions in the Soviet Union. It would contaminate the whole world with the anti-democratic peculiarities of Soviet society. It would enable the Soviet Union to bypass problems it cannot resolve on its own and to concentrate on accumulating further strength. As a result, the world would become disarmed and helpless while facing our uncontrollable bureaucratic apparatus. I think that if rapprochement were to proceed totally without qualifications, on Soviet terms, it would pose a serious threat to the world as a whole.

*In what way?*

It would mean cultivation and encouragement of a closed country, where everything that happens may be shielded from outside eyes, a country wearing a mask that hides its true face. I would not wish it on anyone to live next to such a neighbor, especially if he is at the same time armed to the teeth. I think that most of the political leaders in the West understand the situation, at least the Helsinki Conference seemed to suggest an awareness that rapprochement must be associated with simultaneous liquidation of [Soviet] isolation. Adoption of the Jackson Amendment [by the United States Senate, linking easier trade to unrestricted emigration from the Soviet Union] strikes me as a minimal step that would be significant not only by itself, but also as a symbolic expression of the view that rapprochement must involve some sort of control to insure that this country will not become a threat to its neighbors. As for the emigration of Jews . . .

*Excuse me, the Jackson Amendment does not refer specifically to Jews. It deals with freedom of emigration as such.*

I know, but the Jackson Amendment is often cited in the context of Jewish emigration. Such a narrowing of the issue is very useful to Soviet propaganda, although it is, of course, quite misleading. I do not mean to belittle the Jewish emigration problem in any way. It has been an important, and totally justified, phenomenon in Soviet life, which derives from many factors in the history of the Jewish people and from conditions in the Soviet Union. But the emigration problem is, of course, much broader than that.

*But what would happen if, say, 10 to 20 percent of Soviet scientists decided they wanted to emigrate?*

In the first place, I don't think that the idea would ever occur to even ten percent. The premise is not realistic. But,

in general, it is quite natural for scientists to want to move
from country to country. A lot is being written about the
brain drain, but in fact it does not lead to any catastrophic
consequences. Science is international. Technology, too, is
becoming international, and the place of residence of any
particular scientist should become a matter of personal
choice.

*With regard to forthcoming trials, do you know when
they might begin and why such trials would be staged in
the first place?*

Apparently some trials are scheduled for the near future, maybe in September, judging from indirect indica-
tions.

*What trials are you referring to?*

Yakir and Krasin. The trials have apparently been postponed a number of times. We do not know what preparation may have been necessary. It is hard for me to predict
how they will finally turn out; probably plans have been
changed several times. The point that will evidently be
made is that the activities of Yakir, Krasin, and their associates were used for anti-Soviet purposes by anti-Soviet
organizations. What I said in the introductory statement
today reflects my own point of view on that issue.

*Have you had any news about Grigorenko [retired
Maj. Gen. Pyotr G. Grigorenko, committed to a mental institution in 1969]?*

The news is that there has been no news. He is still in
Chernyakhovsk [Kaliningrad Province, the former East
Prussia] under horrible conditions, and although he was to

have been transferred to a normal hospital by decision of an appeals court, the transfer is being postponed. When his wife inquired about the reasons for the delay, she was told that the director of the present hospital, Bochkov, was away and would be back on September 1. We still hope that Grigorenko will be transferred. That would make it a bit easier for him. He has been undergoing horrible sufferings for the last four years.

*One final question. What specific reasons led you to call this news conference?*

I felt that my summons to the Prosecutor's office contained a certain threat both for me and for members of my family. And then I felt that my conversation there had raised several important issues that required further clarification.

*August 21, 1973*

# A CLARIFICATION

The newspaper campaign [in the Soviet Union] with respect to my recent interviews employs as its fundamental argument the accusation that I am supposedly speaking against the relaxation of international tension, almost in favor of war. This is an unscrupulous play on the anti-war feelings of the nation that suffered the most from the Second World War, that lost millions of its sons and daughters. This is a deliberate distortion of my position.

Beginning in 1958 I have spoken out both in print and in private for ending nuclear tests in the atmosphere. I believe these efforts made their contribution to the conclusion in 1963 of the historic Moscow Treaty banning tests in three environments.

In my fundamental public statements—my *Progress, Coexistence, and Intellectual Freedom* "Memorandum" and

"Postscript"—I have written about elimination of the mortal danger of thermonuclear war as the main problem facing mankind. Therefore I have always welcomed and welcome now the relaxation of international tension and the efforts of governments toward rapprochement of states, toward limitation of the arms race, toward elimination of mutual mistrust. I have believed and believe now that the only real way to solve world problems is the movement of each side toward the other, the convergence of the capitalist and socialist systems accompanied by demilitarization, re-inforcement of the social protection for workers' rights, and creation of a mixed type of economy.

This has been my consistent position and it was re-stated again in my recent interviews with foreign corre-spondents in Moscow. In these interviews I also empha-sized the importance of mutual trust, which requires extensive public disclosure and an open society, democra-tization, free dissemination of information, the exchange of ideas, and respect for all the fundamental rights of the individual—in particular, respect for everyone's right to choose the country in which he wishes to live.

I call attention to the danger of a supposed détente not accompanied by increased trust and democratization. I consider this warning my right and my duty. Is this warn-ing really a statement against détente?

I am speaking up for the trampled rights of my friends in camps and psychiatric hospitals, for Shikhanovich, Bukovsky, Grigorenko, Plyushch, Amalrik, Borisov, Fain-berg, Strkata, and many others. I cannot consider these statements slanders of our system as the newspapers de-scribe them. I deem it important that human rights in our country should be afforded no worse protection than in the countries entering into new, more friendly relations with us, that our towns, our countryside, and our internal life be open, as in those countries, to foreigners and our own citizens as well, including such institutions as places of confinement, psychiatric hospitals, and places of residence and work of those freed on probation. Let the presence of the Red Cross lead to the removal of iron shutters from the windows of Soviet prisons and stay the hand of the criminals who gave haloperidol to Leonid Plyushch in the hell of Dnepropetrovsk prison psychiatric hospital.

The newspaper campaign involving hundreds of persons, among them many honest and intelligent individuals, has deeply grieved me as still another manifestation of brutal coercion of conscience in our nation, coercion based on the unrestricted material and ideological power of the state.

I believe not my statement, but just this newspaper campaign, so foolish and so savage with respect to its participants, can harm international détente.

*September 12, 1973*

# A LETTER TO THE CONGRESS OF THE UNITED STATES

At a time when the Congress is debating fundamental issues of foreign policy, I consider it my duty to express my view on one such issue—the protection of the right to freedom of residence within the country of one's choice. That right was proclaimed by the United Nations in 1948 in the Universal Declaration of Human Rights.

If every nation is entitled to choose the political system under which it wishes to live, this is true all the more of every individual person. A country whose citizens are deprived of this minimal right is not free even if there were not a single citizen who would want to exercise that right.

But, as you know, there are tens of thousands of citizens in the Soviet Union—Jews, Germans, Russians, Ukrainians, Lithuanians, Armenians, Estonians, Latvians, Turks, and members of other ethnic groups—who want to leave the country and who have been seeking to exercise that right for years and for decades at the cost of endless difficulty and humiliation.

You know that prisons, labor camps, and mental hospitals are full of people who have sought to exercise this legitimate right.

You surely know the name of the Lithuanian Simas A. Kudirka, who was handed over to the Soviet authorities by an American vessel, as well as the names of the defendants in the tragic 1970 hijacking trial in Leningrad. You know about the victims of the Berlin wall.

There are many more lesser-known victims. Remember them, too.

For decades the Soviet Union has been developing under conditions of intolerable isolation, bringing with it the ugliest consequences. Even a partial preservation of those conditions would be highly perilous for all mankind, for international confidence and détente.

In view of the foregoing, I am appealing to the Congress of the United States to give its support to the Jackson Amendment, which represents in my view and in the view of its sponsors an attempt to protect the right of emigration of citizens in countries that are entering into new and friendlier relations with the United States.

The Jackson Amendment is made even more significant by the fact that the world is just entering on a new course of détente and it is therefore essential that the proper direction be followed from the outset. This is a fundamental issue, extending far beyond the question of emigration.

Those who believe that the Jackson Amendment is likely to undermine anyone's personal or governmental prestige are wrong. Its provisions are minimal and not demeaning.

It should be no surprise that the democratic process

can add its corrective to the actions of public figures who negotiate without admitting the possibility of such an amendment. The amendment does not represent interference in the internal affairs of socialist countries, but simply a defense of international law, without which there can be no mutual trust.

Adoption of the amendment therefore cannot be a threat to Soviet-American relations. All the more, it would not imperil international détente.

There is a particular silliness in objections to the amendment that are founded on the alleged fear that its adoption would lead to outbursts of anti-Semitism in the USSR and hinder the emigration of Jews.

Here you have total confusion, either deliberate or based on ignorance, about the USSR. It is as if the emigration issue affected only Jews. As if the situation of those Jews who have vainly sought to emigrate to Israel were not already tragic enough and would become even more hopeless if it were to depend on the democratic attitudes and on the humanity of OVIR [the Soviet visa agency]. As if the techniques of "quiet diplomacy" could help anyone, beyond a few individuals in Moscow and some other cities.

The abandonment of a policy of principle would be a betrayal of the thousands of Jews and non-Jews who want to emigrate, of the hundreds in camps and mental hospitals, of the victims of the Berlin wall.

Such a denial would lead to stronger repressions on ideological grounds. It would be tantamount to total capitulation of democratic principles in the face of blackmail, deceit, and violence. The consequences of such a capitulation for international confidence, détente, and the entire future of mankind are difficult to predict.

I express the hope that the Congress of the United States, reflecting the will and the traditional love of freedom of the American people, will realize its historical responsibility before mankind and will find the strength to rise above temporary partisan considerations of commercialism and prestige.

I hope that the Congress will support the Jackson Amendment.

*September 14, 1973*

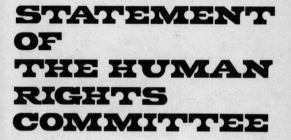

# STATEMENT OF THE HUMAN RIGHTS COMMITTEE

The Committee once again draws the attention of public opinion to the continuing use of psychiatric institutions for political ends in our country. The Committee notes that persons prosecuted in connection with their convictions are, as frequently as before or indeed more frequently, being ruled mentally ill and sent for compulsory treatment, mainly to special prison hospitals. We are firmly convinced that in the overwhelming majority of cases there are no medical grounds for such measures.

Our conviction is based on a great deal of direct and indirect evidence. The very fact of the exceptionally wide-spread occurrence of this form of repression is highly indicative. In a number of cases we have documentary evidence, and in other cases reliable oral testimony, that it is precisely the person's opinions and nothing else that are viewed by experts as evidence of illness. In numerous cases copies of the official psychiatric reports are available, and these can themselves be regarded as proof of such a biased and unscrupulous approach.

A collection of such reports was sent to the West earlier by Bukovsky, who quickly became a victim of judicial revenge for this revelation. We should also mention here that the psychiatrist Gluzman has become another victim of judicial revenge. Reports indicate that the reason was his authorship of an anonymous *in absentia* report on the Grigorenko case. Such acts of revenge for public disclosure are also indicative.

We think it very important that we ourselves personally know many of those who have been declared ill, and in these cases, on the basis of our personal observation as corroborated by their wholly normal life and work, we are convinced of their mental health.

The Committee recalls the names of some of the individuals who have been declared mentally ill for political motives: Grigorenko, Fainberg, Borisov, Gershuni, Ubozhke, Shikhanovich, Plyushch, Starchik, Lupynis, Belov, Kukobaka, Lysak, Mukhamedyarov, Zheleznov, Montlevich, Butkus, and Lavrev.

The Committee notes that persons sent for compulsory treatment have no protection in practice against nonobjective psychiatric examinations, against unfounded, unlimited extension of their hospitalization, against arbitrariness, against harsh and humiliating treatment. Their right to defend their beliefs, and the lawfulness of their actions founded on those beliefs, turn out to be violated, as the court, acting moreover in their absence, regards these beliefs as both evidence of and a consequence of their mental illness.

The Committee urges the following:

1. Demand that relatives of persons undergoing psychiatric examination have the right to select psychiatric experts of their choice, including the right to request foreign psychiatric experts, especially in cases attracting public attention and in cases where a basis exists to doubt the objectivity of the examination; and demand, in particular, examination by a commission of experts, including foreign psychiatrists for the persons named above.

2. Demand—when the public becomes concerned about the use of psychiatry for repressive purposes in any country or about harsh treatment insulting to the dignity of mentally ill persons—the formation of an international commission organized by WHO [the World Health Organization], the Red Cross, and other international organizations and including psychiatrists. In particular, regard as essential the international investigation of the special psychiatric hospitals of the USSR Ministry of Internal Affairs in Dnepropetrovsk, Sychevka, Orel, Kazan, Leningrad, and Chernyakhovsk.

3. Recommend to foreign psychiatric agencies and organizations that they insistently request the transfer of some patients from Soviet psychiatric hospitals, including special hospitals, for observation in foreign hospitals and, if necessary, for treatment there; in particular, insist on the transfer of the individuals named above.

4. Organize in international and national psychiatric organizations discussion of the state of Soviet psychiatry, and, in particular, discussion of the personal role of the psychiatrists who serve on commissions in political cases.

The Committee appeals to international and national psychiatric organizations and asks for discussion and support of the proposals listed above, and also for constructive counterproposals. The Committee calls on psychiatrists throughout the world to speak out in defense of their colleague Semyon Gluzman and of Vladimir Bukovsky.

ANDREI  SAKHAROV
GRIGORY  PODYAPOLSKY
IGOR  SHAFAREVICH

*October 1, 1973*

# INTERVIEW WITH A LEBANESE CORRESPONDENT

The events in the Near East alarm me greatly. I do not know if words can be important at such a moment but I am ready to answer your questions.

*How do you appraise the events in the Near East?*

This war, which began with simultaneous large-scale Egyptian and Syrian military operations, is a great tragedy both for Arabs and for Jews. But for Israel in this war, just as in the wars of 1949, 1956, and 1967, what is at stake is the very existence of the state, the right to life. I believe that for the Arabs this war is basically a result of the play of internal and external political forces, of considerations of prestige, of nationalistic prejudices. I believe that this difference exists and must be taken into account when appraising these events.

*What can the Arabs and Israelis do to end this conflict?*

Immediately agree to a cease-fire and sit down to negotiations. The Arabs should clearly and unequivocally declare that they recognize Israel's right to existence within borders insuring its military security, fundamental economic interests, and prospective immigration. Israel should give guarantees in return. With these conditions the honorable peace long wished for by both parties is possible.

*What steps can the United States and Western nations take to terminate the war?*

Call upon the USSR and socialist countries to abandon the policy of one-sided interference in the Arab-Israeli conflict, and take retaliatory measures if this policy of interference continues. Use all means, including diplomatic, for an immediate cease-fire and for the initiation of direct peace negotiations between the Arabs and Israel. Make effective use of the United Nations Charter to safeguard peace and security.

*Which is better for socialist countries and countries of the third world—an Israeli victory or an Arab victory?*

The people of all countries are interested not in military victories but in peace and security, in respect for the rights and hopes of all nationalities, in tolerance and in freedom.

*How can you, as a defender of human rights, help the Arab countries?*

I speak out for the democratization of life in our country, and this is closely related to our foreign policy and the relaxation of international tensions. The Arab countries, as countries throughout the world, have an interest in this as one of the conditions for development free from external forces.

*At the present time do you intend to criticize the policy of Israel's leaders?*

No. That country, which is the realization of the Jewish people's right to a state, is today fighting for its existence surrounded by enemies who exceed it in population and material resources many times over. This hostility was stirred up to a considerable extent by the imprudent policies of other states. All mankind has on its conscience the Jewish victims of Nazi genocide during the Second World War. We cannot permit a repetition of that tragedy today.

*October 11, 1973*

# STATEMENT ON RECEIVING THE AWARD OF THE INTERNATIONAL LEAGUE FOR THE RIGHTS OF MAN

I accept this prize with deep gratitude and emotion.

I am thinking at this moment of hundreds of my friends and people of like persuasion who are in camps, prisons, and psychiatric hospitals and who, through their courage and suffering, are affirming the defense of human rights as a supreme goal of society.

In 1948 the United Nations adopted a great humanistic document of the era—the Universal Declaration of Human Rights. The UN thereby took upon itself the defense of human rights in every country. In those years the Stalinist dictatorship was committing unprecedented crimes in our country, trampling human rights underfoot at every step. Now times have changed in many respects. But as before, the international defense of human rights is very important to the citizens of our country. Still unsolved are problems of great importance to the spiritual, political, and economic health of society, such as assuring freedom of one's convictions and conscience, assuring public disclosure, freedom of the press and information. Still unsolved are many problems of national equality. The Crimean Tatars, the Volga Germans, and the Meskhi Turks, resettled under the Stalinist tyranny, cannot return to their homelands. Such a key problem for our country as that of assuring freedom of emigration is still unsolved.

I would like to believe that the awarding to a Soviet citizen of the International Human Rights Prize demonstrates that international attention to assuring human rights in our country will increase and have a deep influence.

A. SAKHAROV

*December 5, 1973*

[*Read on behalf of Andrei Sakharov by his representative, Dr. Herman Feschbach, at a session of the International League for the Rights of Man.*]

# DECLARATION ON SOLZHENITSYN

We are deeply perturbed and exasperated by the new threats to Alexander Solzhenitsyn contained in a recent Tass statement. Tass declares that Solzhenitsyn is a "traitor to the Motherland" who libels its past. But how is it possible to affirm that the "mistakes made" have been condemned and corrected and, at the same time, to characterize as libel an honest attempt to gather and publish historical and folkloric information on a part of those crimes that burden our collective conscience? After all, it cannot be denied that there actually were mass arrests, tortures, executions, forced labor, inhuman conditions, and the deliberate annihilation of millions of people in camps. There was the dispossession of the kulaks, the persecution and annihilation of hundreds of thousands of believers, forcible resettling of peoples, anti-worker and anti-peasant laws, and the persecution of those who had returned from prisoner-of-war camps. And there were other crimes whose harshness, perfidy, and cynicism were astounding.

The right of an author to write and publish that which is dictated by his conscience and duty as an artist is one of the most basic in civilized society. This right cannot be limited by national boundaries. *A fortiori*, the opportunity to set such limits cannot be given to the All-Union Agency for the Protection of Copyright, that allegedly social organization which in fact performs the functions of political censorship and currency speculation on an author's work.

We are convinced there are no legal grounds for prosecuting* Solzhenitsyn for his having published his new book, *The Gulag Archipelago*, abroad, just as there are no grounds for prosecuting anyone for similar acts. We know, however, that in our state prosecutions are possible even without such grounds. We call upon honest people throughout the world to resist this danger—to protect the pride of Russian and world culture, Alexander Solzhenitsyn.

ANDREI SAKHAROV
ALEXANDER GALICH
VLADIMIR MAXIMOV
VLADIMIR VOINOVICH
IGOR SHAFAREVICH

*January 5, 1974*

* Also translatable as "persecuting." [Translator's note.]

# APPENDIX

APPEAL TO THE GENERAL SECRETARY OF THE CENTRAL
COMMITTEE AND THE USSR PROSECUTOR GENERAL

I ask you to use your influence and authority to have
the sentence passed on Vladimir Bukovsky set aside and
Bukovsky himself released. . . . It is in the interests of the
healthy elements of the leadership of the country and
among our people that this unjust sentence should be set
aside, and in a broader context that this country, which has
endured so much suffering and degradation, should undergo a moral regeneration. For only the moral health of the
people is a true guarantee of the viability of the country in
creative labor and in the face of coming trials.

Restore legality and justice!

*January 18, 1972*

TO: THE HUMAN RIGHTS COMMITTEE

FROM: COMMITTEE MEMBER A. D. SAKHAROV

ON THE PROBLEM OF RESTORING THE RIGHTS OF
PERSONS AND PEOPLES VIOLATED IN THE COURSE
OF FORCIBLE RESETTLEMENT.

The Committee has received documents from representatives of the Crimean Tatar people and the Meskhi-Turkic people in which the Committee's attention is drawn to the important problem of restoring the rights of persons and peoples violated in the course of resettlement. The Committee is aware that a situation requiring the restoration of rights also exists with respect to the Volga German people.

I propose that the Committee consider the following problems:

1. The circumstances of the forcible resettlement of peoples—Volga Germans, Kalmyks, Circassians, Karachai, Balkars, Crimean Tatars, Meskhi, Greeks, and also the Koreans resettled before the war.

2. An analysis of the violations of legality and humanity committed in the course of forcible resettlement.

3. The circumstances of the forcible detention of resettled persons in their places of residence, the presence of special commandant's offices and other extralegal restrictions on rights, aggravating the already frightful situation of the resettled persons and leading to mass mortality.

4. An analysis of the situation existing at the present moment; in particular, discriminatory restrictions as regards residence permits, employment, education, the right to acquire property, etc., vis-à-vis the Crimean Tatars, the Volga Germans, and the Meskhi.

5. a) An analysis of the causes which led the Stalinist administration to commit the crimes of genocide named in paragraphs 1, 2, and 3.

    b) An analysis of the causes conducive to delays in the restoration of the rights of resettled persons at the present time.

I propose that we discuss the role of the following factors: the role of the general–ideological course of great-power chauvinism; visible violence as a means of the political manipulation of prejudices and low instincts; the role of economic and social factors; the role of the general political and psychological situation in a time of war.

6. The persecution of persons who have supported the restoration of the rights of resettled peoples.

7. What *démarches* and documents of the Committee might help in the resolution of the problem.

*March 16, 1972*

### TO THE PRESIDIUM OF THE SUPREME SOVIET USSR

At the request of interested parties, the Human Rights Committee has familiarized itself with the problem of restoring the rights of forcibly resettled peoples and ethnic groups. While expressing satisfaction at the restoration of the rights of several such peoples, we call upon the Presidium of the Supreme Soviet to help restore the rights of the Crimean Tatars and the Meskhi (and other peoples and groups) to live on the territory from which they were forcibly and illegally resettled.

We call upon the Presidium of the Supreme Soviet to

take steps to see that all citizens of our country can fully exercise their right freely to choose a place of residence; that in particular this right can be exercised by citizens of these nationalities pending general settlement of the question of the return of their territory to them: to settle on that territory, to acquire housing, and to work.

A. D. SAKHAROV

A. N. TVERDOKHLEBOV

V. N. CHALIDZE

I. R. SHAFAREVICH

*April 21, 1972*

*These two petitions, drafted and circulated by Andrei Sakharov and signed by more than fifty Soviet intellectuals, were sent to the USSR Supreme Soviet in autumn, 1972.*

### TO THE USSR SUPREME SOVIET: AN APPEAL FOR AMNESTY

In the anniversary year of the formation of the Union of the Soviet Socialist Republics, we call on you to adopt decisions that correspond in their humanity and democratic thrust to the fundamental interests of our society.

We call on you to adopt, among such decisions, a law on amnesty.

We believe that this law should provide particularly for the release of those convicted for reasons directly or indirectly connected with their beliefs and specifically: those convicted under Articles 190-3 and Articles 70 and 72 of the RSFSR Criminal Code, and under the corresponding articles of the Codes of other Union Republics; all those convicted in connection with their religious beliefs; and all those convicted in connection with an attempt to leave the country. We call on you also to review the decisions made on similar grounds to confine people in special "prison" or ordinary psychiatric hospitals.

Freedom of conscience and freedom to express and defend one's opinions are each man's inalienable rights. These freedoms are, moreover, a guarantee of a society's vitality.

We also consider that a law on amnesty, in conformity with juridical norms and humanity, should provide for the release of all individuals who have served a term of imprisonment in excess of the present maximum of fifteen years on the basis of sentences pronounced before the adoption of the Fundamental Principles of Legislation now in force.

TO THE USSR SUPREME SOVIET: ON ABOLITION OF THE
DEATH PENALTY

Many people have long sought the abolition of the death penalty, believing that it contradicts moral sensibility and cannot be justified by any general social considerations. The death penalty has now been abolished in many countries.

On the anniversary of the formation of the Union of Soviet Socialist Republics, we call on the USSR Supreme Soviet to adopt a law abolishing the death penalty in our country.

Such a decision would promote the extension of this humane act throughout the world.

## [*Telegram*]

TO L. I. BREZHNEV, GENERAL SECRETARY OF THE CC CPSU

TWO YEARS AGO I ADDRESSED MYSELF TO YOU IN CONNECTION
WITH THE CASE OF FRIEDRICH RUPPEL, WHO WANTED TO BE
REPATRIATED WITH HIS FAMILY TO THE FEDERAL GERMAN
REPUBLIC. IN 1941 HIS MOTHER WAS SHOT ON THE BASIS OF
A FALSE CHARGE. HE HIMSELF, AS A BOY, SPENT TEN YEARS IN
A CAMP AS THE RESULT OF A SENTENCE BY AN OSO.* TODAY,
THE DAY OF YOUR ARRIVAL IN BONN, AFTER FOUR YEARS OF
EFFORTS, RUPPEL'S REQUEST WAS REFUSED. I ASK YOU TO IN-
TERVENE AND PUT AN END TO VIOLATIONS OF HUMAN RIGHTS
WHICH DO DAMAGE TO THE PRESTIGE OF OUR NATION.

RESPECTFULLY,

SAKHAROV, ACADEMICIAN

*May 18, 1973*

TO THE SECRETARY-GENERAL OF THE UN, MR. KURT WALD-
HEIM

In 1968–9 several Soviet citizens who were endeavoring,
from a position loyal to the state, to defend victims of un-
lawful repressions, submitted detailed protests to your
predecessor in the post of Secretary-General of the UN. In
subsequent years the majority of these people, who call
themselves the Initiative Group for the Defense of Human
Rights, have themselves become the victims of equally un-

* A "special conference [board]," or "troika," of the secret police.
[Translator's note.]

lawful repressions. We consider the defense of these people a duty of the organization that proclaimed the Universal Declaration of Human Rights, and a matter involving its prestige.

In this appeal we ask you to come forward in defense of two members of the Initiative Group who have been sentenced to an especially terrible fate—indefinite incarceration in a psychiatric prison. We refer to Vladimir Borisov, arrested in 1969, who has already languished for more than three years in a Leningrad special [i.e., administered by the MVD] prison-type hospital; and Leonid Plyushch, arrested in January of 1972. The investigation and trial of their cases abounded with impermissible violations of legal norms—in particular, of the right to public disclosure and the right to a defense—and in violation of medical ethics. The public is aware of Borisov's heroic struggle and his prolonged political hunger strikes, together with Victor Fainberg, for the right to a hearing in court. This struggle has provoked unconcealed hatred toward Borisov on the part of those in whose hands he finds himself.

At the present time we are especially alarmed about the fate of the Kiev mathematician Leonid Plyushch. His case has been characterized by determined efforts at concealment that are unusual even under our conditions, and that compel one to surmise a desire to conceal even more serious violations of the law. Plyushch's trial took place in an empty hall in the absence of the accused and his representative. Defense counsel had only one brief meeting with his client. The court, basing its decision on an experts' report that was not read out during the hearing, and that, moreover, was drawn up without any personal examination of Plyushch, sent him to a special psychiatric hospital. The

appeals court mitigated this decision, changing the type of
hospital. However, even though this decision has now entered into legal force, Plyushch is still in an investigation
prison of the KGB; and his wife is not allowed to visit her
husband, whom she has not seen for a year and a half. Recently, in accordance with a protest lodged by the prosecutor's office, a new appellate review was ordered, so that
Plyushch is again threatened with a special hospital. No
results have been forthcoming from the numerous appeals
made to individual authorities and Soviet agencies in connection with the Borisov and Plyushch cases.

We ask you to come forward in defense of Vladimir
Borisov and Leonid Plyushch. This is important in order to
not only save these individuals and lessen the tragedy of
those close to them but also prevent similar violations of
human rights in our country.

We attach a letter from T. Khodorovich, a member of
the Initiative Group, which contains important details on
the case of L. I. Plyushch.

Respectfully,

ANDREI SAKHAROV

GRIGORY PODYAPOLSKY

*Moscow*
*June 25, 1973*

APPEAL TO THE CHILEAN GOVERNMENT ABOUT PABLO
NERUDA

Worried about the fate of the outstanding contemporary poet and winner of the Nobel Prize for Literature,
Pablo Neruda, we appeal to you to fulfill the duties of the

position you have occupied and to safeguard the freedom and security of your remarkable citizen. One may agree or not agree with his world view and political position, but by his whole life and creative work he has proved to mankind the sincerity and purity of the beliefs he has propounded.

Pablo Neruda is not only a great Chilean poet but also the pride of all Latin-American literature. His glorious name is indissolubly bound up with the struggle of the peoples of Latin America for their spiritual and national liberation. The violent death of this great man would darken for a long time what your Government has proclaimed as the rebirth and consolidation of Chile.

Humanity and magnanimity on your part to one of your best fellow countrymen would undoubtedly promote normalization and relaxation of tensions both in your own country and in the whole world.

ANDREI SAKHAROV<br>ALEXANDER GALICH<br>VLADIMIR MAXIMOV

*September 18, 1973*

## IN SUPPORT OF THE APPEAL OF THE INTERNATIONAL COMMITTEE FOR THE DEFENSE OF HUMAN RIGHTS

The proposals of the International Committee aimed at creating conditions for the free exchange of people and ideas between the countries of the West and the socialist countries, free tourism, free choice of country of residence, free exchange of books, manuscripts, films, and other things

of cultural value are extremely important. The implementation of these proposals would create a new situation
in the world—one in which mutual understanding and trust
would rule out the possibility of military conflicts. The
implementation of these proposals is impossible without
strong pressure by the peoples on their own governments
and those of all European countries, including the governments of the countries of eastern Europe. I call upon all
honest people throughout the world to support the proposals of the International Committee for the Defense of
Human Rights, and to help with their efforts to realize
them.

ANDREI SAKHAROV, ACADEMICIAN

*Moscow*
*December 29, 1973*